A Bard's Day's Night
('s Dream)

or

Stratford Upon Avon Calling

or

A Bunch of B.S.
(Bill Shakespeare)

or

Shakespearean Rhapsody

or

How I Learned to Stop Worrying
and Love the Bard

by Jory Levine

*This play's story and characters are based on those depicted
in works by William Shakespeare. The character of King Milhous
is not based on Richard M. Nixon...or is it?*

*All images used in this publication have been digitally altered.
Most are in the public domain. Copyrighted visual material
appears within these pages in accordance with the
Fair Use Doctrine; Section 107 of the Copyright Act of 1976,
in the service of social commentary and parody.
Dude, don't be a dick about it.*

*All rights reserved.
Copyright © 2018 by Jory Levine
Library of Congress Catalog Number: PA0001340012
No part of this publication may be reproduced or transmitted
in any form or by any means, electronic or mechanical
including photocopying, recording, or by any information
storage and retrieval system without permission in
writing from the publisher, except in the case of
brief quotations embodied in critical reviews
and certain other noncommercial uses
permitted by copyright law.*

ISBN 978-1-7329800-0-6

PRINTED IN THE UNITED STATES OF AMERICA

THE PERSONS OF THE PLAY

SCHMUCK, a woodland creature

ROSENSTERN & GUILDENCRANTZ, palace guards

The GHOST, spirit of Hameo's father

HAMEO, son of Queen Patsy and King Hyperius

The Duke of BILGEWATER, friend to Milhous

KING MILHOUS, uncle of Hameo

THELONIOUS, father of Lymetrius

LYMETRIUS, a Moorish friend to Hameo

QUEEN PATSY, wife of King Milhous

The TWO AND A HALF WITCHES, a fortune-telling coven

BAWDY MEN, patrons of Fatstaff's inn

FATSTAFF, an innkeeper

BARKEEP, Fatstaff's barman

ABIGAIL & ELOISE, bar wenches

HEMLOCK, a cannibal

JULINIA, daughter of King Bolingbras

HIPPOPOTIMA, handmaiden to Julinia

KING BOLINGBRAS, nemesis of King Milhous

The PLAYWRIGHT, a bard

The PLAYERS, Tog Dog, Q-Tip, Hashpipe, Snuggy Bear, Snotrag, Starvin' Marvin

AUDIENCE MEMBERS, Puerto Rican, Asian, Irishman, Englishman, Jew, German, Frenchman

MUSKRAT, friend to Schmuck

The MAGISTRATE

A Bard's Day's Night ('s Dream) opened on September 7, 2006 at The American Theatre of Actors - Chernuchen Theatre, New York City, New York. The play was produced by Jory Levine with the following cast:

CAST OF CHARACTERS
(in order of appearance)

SCHMUCK	Johnathan Lang
ROSENSTERN/ENGLISHMAN	John Bertrand
GUILDENCRANTZ/GERMAN	Nick Fondulis
GHOST/BAWDY MAN/PUERTO RICAN	Daniel Kemna
HAMEO	Dan Rice
BILGEWATER/IRISHMAN/MAGISTRATE	Joshua Levine
KING MILHOUS	Joel Altherr
THELONIOUS/BAWDY MAN/PLAYWRIGHT/SERVANT	Jory Levine
LYMETRIUS	Skyih S. Smith
QUEEN PATSY	Wendy Charles
THE FIRST WITCH/ABIGAIL	Morgan Jae
THE SECOND WITCH/ELOISE	Heather Wildenberger
THE HALF WITCH/FRENCHMAN	Kristen Dodson
FATSTAFF	John D'Arcangelo
HEMLOCK	Henrik Petersen
JULINIA	Aimee McCabe
HIPPOPOTIMA	Tina Barone
BOLINGBRAS/BAWDY MAN	John Scamardella
TOP DOG	Torre Reigns
Q-TIP	Russel Jordan
HASHPIPE	William Sudan Mason
SNOTRAG	Ledwin Lopez
SNUGGY BEAR/BARKEEP/BOLINGBRAS'S SERVANT	Alan Pagano
STARVIN' MARVIN	David Harrison
ASIAN/MILHOUS'S SERVANT/BAWDY MAN	Frank Lin
MUSKRAT	Shruti Shah

Director/Set Designer	Jory Levine
Lighting Designer	Alexander Casagrande
Stage Manager	Jonathan Deutsch
Assistant Stage Manager	Erin Sromierski

The action takes place in the 16th Century...somewhere in Europe.

A Bard's Day's Night
('s Dream)

ACT I

1.1 We are introduced to Schmuck, a mischievous woodland creature that will multi-functionally serve as narrator, comic relief and deus ex machina over the course of the play. While Shakespeare's Puck is oft depicted as a saytr-like elf or sprite, our embodiment possesses the fluffy ears of a rabbit, one winged arm of a parrot, furry legs and the feet of a coyote.

---

5. **A good fellow to be sure**: The Puck in *A Midsummer Night's Dream* was named Robin Goodfellow.

1.2 Rosenstern and Guildencrantz, the palace guards, have summoned and await Prince Hameo, as their night watch has been haunted by the ghost of what they believe to be Hameo's father, the former king, Hyperius. Hameo discovers from the ghost that his uncle, and now king, Milhous, killed his father by providing him with a wench that had a deadly venereal disease so that he may assume the throne and have his mother, Queen Patsy, as his wife. Hameo vows to his father that he will avenge his death but questions his own resolve to complete the task.

ACT I

1.1 *Enter Schmuck, a woodland creature.*

SCHMUCK
Good morrow to you one and all.
But soft, fear not.
Be not in huff o'er mine hoof.
I am but a woodland puck, Schmuck by name—
A good fellow to be sure. 5
Though my form be of beast,
My heart is good and kind
And I have it in my mind to impart to thee a tale;
In part of love and treachery,
In part of greed, and if you please, of lechery. 10
So let me be your guide
And together we shall glide through this weavéd plot,
Entangled tales as yet unmeshed.
And if thou be of Rome or home of Scots or Budapest,
It makes no mind. All shall be revealed 15
And all in good time.

[*Exit.*]

1.2 *Enter Guildencrantz and Rosenstern,
the palace guards.*

ROSENSTERN
What ho, Guildencrantz!

GUILDENCRANTZ
Ahh! Rosenstern, thou did'st scare the fecal matter
From mine entrails.

ROSENSTERN
I merely come to relieve thee of thy watch,
Not give thee cause to relieve thyself in'st thine armor. 5

GUILDENCRANTZ
Care I not the state of mine undergarb,
When low these past three nights,

8. **former lord and king, Hyperius:** Many of the character names that appear in *A Bard's Day's Night ('s Dream)* are either an amalgam, homage or allusion to character names that Shakespeare himself used in his cannon of plays. The name *Hyperius* may not be readily apparent to those familiar with Shakespeare's work. It is derived from a line in *Hamlet:* "So excellent a king; that was, to this, Hyperion to a satyr." Here, Hamlet likens his father to the Greek mythological Titan, the son of earth and sky, and compares him to the satyr that is Claudius, who killed his father and took his throne and wife.

The vaporous form of our former lord and king, Hyperius,
Doth haunt the watch of which I'd switch
With any fool with valor's itch. 10

ROSENSTERN
I be that fool. Calm thee, sir!
Thou dost discredit to thy service
And all that serve with thee.
Show me this vaporous villain.
With saber I will re-tailor his cloudy shroud. 15
Thus and thus and thus.

GUILDENCRANTZ
Brave words indeed.
But we shall see upon the stroke of twelve,
When evil will arise from whence it dwells,
If bold words have the companionship of action. 20
The hour sounds. Look ho, it comes anon!

GHOST (O.S.)
Oooooh!!

ROSENSTERN
By heaven,
What spawn of hell comes hither
To pluck our very souls? 25
Oh! I fear I did as thou did'st do.

GUILDENCRANTZ
Number 1?

ROSENSTERN
And number 2.

Enter Hameo.

HAMEO
Guildencrantz. I have come upon the hour
Twixt the days at your behest. 30

GUILDENCRANTZ
And just in time, my liege.
Though time be not just to thy phantom father,
Who stolen too soon from earth is drawn back to't
With words of gravity for thine ear.

35. **Scrameth you from here:** to leave or go away from a place quickly (Other synonymous phrases: "beat it"; "take a hike"; "skedaddle"; "get lost"; "scoot" or otherwise "fuck off.")

43. **Cry havoc and let slip the discs of your...back:** This is a reference to the line is Shakespeare's *Julius Caesar* in which Marc Anthony imagines Caesar calling for vengeance over his assassination—"Cry havoc, and let slip the dogs of war." Of course, the success of such an endeavor would largely be determined by how loud the cry was and, obviously, the size of the dogs. If, on the day in question, you had laryngitis and a grouping of three Pomeranians and a Shih Tzu, your desire for revenge may go largely unfulfilled.

HAMEO
  Scrameth you from here, good friends. 35
  I will have audience with this odious apparition.

ROSENSTERN
  Thou needst not prithee twice.
  Come Guildencrantz, away.

  [Exeunt Rosenstern and Guildencrantz.]

HAMEO
  O, intemperate spirit. Reveal thyself and thy purpose.

  Enter Ghost of Hyperius.

GHOST
  Ooooh. Ooooooh. Ooooooh, mine achin' back. 40

HAMEO
  Sit here upon this stump.

GHOST
  Eternal slumber takes its toll upon my lumbar.

HAMEO
  Cry havoc and let slip the discs of your...back.

GHOST
  Ha ha! My son,
  You e'er didst have a great wit about you. 45
  Use it sometime.

HAMEO
  What brings you hither, father?

GHOST
  O, Hameo, fruit of my loins,
  I know thou loved me well and will hear
  With tristful ears my tale of treachery. 50
  How my brother, thine uncle,
  A carbuncle on the sinew of our lineage,
  Didst with malicious premeditation contrive
  Then execute the circumstance of my demise
  And subsequently took the Lady Patsy for his prize. 55

60. **bated drums:** referring to *eardrums* in anticipation of hearing what Hameo's father has come to tell him. We hear the word *bated* almost exclusively in the phrase *bated breath* but I must ask, cannot other things be moderated or restrained in anticipation? Perhaps "I am waiting to see you with bated eyeballs" or "Roger watched his girlfriend undress with bated penis" or even, "The fishhook dangled in the water with bated bait." Let's get creative, folks!

69. **the goddess Venus did smite:** Venus is, of course, known as the goddess on the mountain top that burned like a silver flame and was the summit of beauty and love...and she's "got it." Also, she's the etymological source for the word *venereal* as in "venereal disease."

86. **I can pee clearly. Now the pain is gone:** *I Can See Clearly Now* (1972) by Johnny Nash—lyric, "I can see clearly now the rain is gone." There is also a 1993 version by Jimmy Cliff, but Johnny holds the word *sky* for 18 seconds in the middle of the song using a single breath and Jimmy craps out after nine seconds and lets his backup singers finish for him. Sorry, Jimmy—no cigar!

HAMEO
   Dear great and gaseous giver of my life,
   If thou hast by some alchemy broke free
   The cold embrace of death to impart to me
   The wisdom of the netherworld, speak thee straight
   As I await thy words with bated drums.   60

GHOST
   Knowing well my carnal desire for
   Feminine acquaintance, thine uncle brought forth
   A winsome wench for my pleasure;
   Making claim her precious treasure
   Was as yet unknown by man.   65
   And yet, known unto him, 'twas not so.
   For the cruel and crafty Milhous proffered a nymph
   So tainted with the touch of loathsome lads
   That the goddess Venus did smite her most sacred region
   And mine own in the course of its conquest.   70
   Yea, even the virility of my majestic scepter
   Was no match for her profound displeasure.
   So this simple strumpet, which me thought so generous,
   Was indeed most ghonerous.
   And thusly, with this disease-laden lass   75
   As his instrument to play his malevolent hand,
   Milhous laid low the lord of the land
   And literally "snatched" my very life away.
   And in the fast passing of time,
   The grapes did wither on the vine.   80
   Affixing an untimely vintage
   To the sweet libation of my life.

HAMEO
   I pray the aliment affects thee not in death
   As't hath on earth.

GHOST
   Oh, no, sweet Hameo.   85
   I can pee clearly. Now the pain is gone.

HAMEO
   O, ill-treated spirit.
   I grieve for the grave injustice thou hast sufferéd
   And swear to thee, while there be air suffice to fill my lung,
   The sweet song of revenge will assuredly be sung.   90

100. **eat thy vegetables:** This is sage advice for Hameo and for us all, by and large. Adding vegetables as a regular part of your daily diet will help to reduce many chronic diseases. They're a great source of many important nutrients, including potassium, fiber, folate (folic acid) and vitamins A, E and C. Eating a diet rich in vegetables is a smart choice and may reduce risk for stroke, cancer, heart disease and Type 2 diabetes. So why not heed the suggestion of a dead king, get thee to a supermarket and grab a few carrots, peppers, onions and some nice leafy greens—you'll be glad you did.

105-7. **Upon my narrow shoulders...Atlas shrug:** *Atlas Shrugged* (1957) by Ayn Rand—brilliant Russian novelist who, unfortunately, could not properly pronounce her own first name; **the cojones to do the dirty deed?:** *Cojones* is Spanish for testicles; nads; brass ones; stones; boys; family jewels; nuts; nards; sweetbreads; goolies and jingle bells. In fact, you will find an entire monologue dedicated to balls on page 139 of this very play. It is true that doing dirty deeds does require cojones of substantial weight and potency but there have been instances in history, for example with Hitler or Lance Armstrong, where a single conjone was sufficient to accomplish truly heinous endeavors.

107-8. **wipe away this duty...assiduous list:** This is a bit of sophisticated wordplay in which the word *duty* is, at once, related to a overt sense of obligation but also, homonymically, refers to the word *doodie* or, if you will, *poopy*, *doo doo*, *caca* or the compound word *cocky-doody*. To add even more complexity, the word *assiduous* is also employed with the first syllable, *ass*, as a gentle reminder to the audience as to the place of origin of the aforementioned doodie.

GHOST
Dear Hameo, the netherworld demands my swift retreat.
There are worms to feed and they must eat.
Return I not of my own volition
But return I must to my decomposition.

HAMEO
Farewell father. You will be avenged; this I avow. 95

GHOST
And Hameo...

HAMEO
Yes, my father?

GHOST
One final word.

HAMEO
Speak it.

GHOST
Forget thee not to eat thy vegetables. Oooooh. 100

[Exit Ghost.]

HAMEO
What a strange and wondrous thing is this?
My heart doth patter-pitter o'er
This rather sweet and bitter reunion.
Can I take the life of he that took my dear dad's wife?
Upon my narrow shoulders this specter placed the onus. 105
Have I the cojones to do the dirty deed?
Or will this Atlas shrug and wipe away this duty
From my assiduous list of obligations?
I now have need for meed and the council
Of my dear friend Lymetrius, 110
Whose help in times of trouble is treble needed now.
O, why should such a fate befall me?
Why should conscience bait and gall me?
Why am I asking you?
Away with me. Questions wait for answer's call. 115
And sate not I till answered all.

[Exit.]

1.3 The evil Duke of Bilgewater is summoned to the palace of King Milhous to help him concoct a plan to rid him of his nephew, Hameo. Bilgewater suggests sending Hameo off to spy on Milhous's foe, King Bolingbras, assuming he will be captured and killed. This will also have the added benefit of allowing Mihous to initiate a war with Bolingbras, using his nephew's death as an excuse. Hameo arrives and questions his uncle about the circumstances of his father's death. Milhous feigns ignorance and recommends the Bolingbras mission as a means to assuage his melancholy and that he should take his good friend Lymetrius along as a companion. Hameo agrees and the trap is set.

Flourish: Throughout the play, a servant will introduce character entrances with a trumpet flourish. Instead of just having a generic melody, each flourish will be a measure or two of contemporary music specifically suited to the character or situation in question.

King Milhous: This character is meant to be a analogue to Shakespeare's Richard III. I decided to take it one step further and had the character portrayed as Richard Milhous Nixon (1913-1994), the esteemed 37th President of the United States.

12. **slings and bows:** Hamlet speaks of "suffering the slings and arrows of outrageous fortune."

15-16. **serpent speed...my aspirations:** Do note, the first syllable of *aspirations* is the word *asp*—a venomous snake of the Nile.

1.3 *Enter Milhous and a Servant with trumpet.*

SERVANT
>*[Flourish: "Smoke on the water..."]*

The Duke of Bilgewater.

>*Enter Bilgewater.*
>>*[Exit the Servant.]*

BILGEWATER
You sent for me, sire?

KING MILHOUS
Arise from your disingenuous genuflection.
You know me well, Bilgewater,
And the disorder I have caused within this realm   5
By grabbing hold the helm from my brother's grasp.
I have taxed the rich, enjoyed their wealth.
Worked peasants raw, destroyed their health.
Kicked puppies' paws to hear their yelps.
I'd even steal a stealer's stealth, if 'twere a possibility.   10
And those that I suppose would take their
Slings and bows and rise against me make me cross.
And so I give them dungeon homes
And heads that roll and gather no moss.
Usurpers ceased with serpent speed;   15
My aspiration, to date, unchecked.
So why the heck I worry so?
Alas, I do confess I do not know.

BILGEWATER
Perchance you sense unrest within
The breast of your young nephew, Hameo.   20
I fear the cat from bag is out.
He may be young but he has clout
And soon his shouts of treason
Will, for retribution, give the reason
For those who do oppose your reign.   25

KING MILHOUS
Bilgewater, my foul friend,
Your rottenness doth rival even mine.

38-46. I did just now confer...suck my caucus: Mihous has a metaphoric meeting with his twenty golden ducats. And at this gathering, they decide that Bilgewater will be their "candidate" if he can devise a plan to eliminate Hameo. Bilgewater takes on the task for the sake of this compensation and wishes to "imbibe" the assemblage, thereby sucking King Milhous's caucus. I liked the sound of "suck my caucus" and worked my way backward to justify it, which just goes to show that you can never go too far in the pursuit of creating of a truly bad blowjob joke; **try my purple patience:** The color purple has been associated with royalty, power, wealth and Whoopie Goldberg for centuries.

> Canst thou divine from the cesspool of thy soul
> Some suitable scheme to rid me of this retched runt
> Who halts my plans and haunts my dreams? 30

BILGEWATER
> Alas, my mind is all a muddle.
> 'Tis not the norm for clouds to rage
> And cause a hazy storm when thinking
> Thoughts of ill and hate.
> Quite commonly I'm sharp and shrewd, 35
> Not prone to discombobulate.

KING MILHOUS
> Thy transparency offends mine intellect.
> I did just now confer with these twenty golden ducats.
> And agreed are we
> That they shall make a home with thee 40
> As but a contribution to our candidate,
> Providing thou no longer try my purple patience
> And put thy temples to the task.

BILGEWATER
> I kneel to thee with gratitude
> As I imbibe this generous assemblage. 45

KING MILHOUS
> O, suck my caucus. (*gives pouch of coins.*)

BILGEWATER
> And thus, as if by alchemy,
> My formerly befoggéd brain doth bubble so
> With horrid harms for Hameo.
> A phalanx filled of fiendish fates 50
> Awaits thy naughty nephew.
> Where to begin? Where to start?
> An errant arrow through his heart?
> His vernal form so fresh and limber
> Crushéd quick by falling timber. 55
> Poisoned berries in his food?
> Boiled in oil's always good.
> The rabid scratchings of a cat?
> A window nudge and then a splat.

67. **We needn't...waste this wascal:** This is an allusion to the famed rifleman and hunting enthusiast, Elmer J. Fudd, whose preferred prey was the *Sylvilagus* or cottontail rabbit—he was also known to be a millionaire with a mansion and a yacht. Fudd suffered from a speech impediment known as *rhotacism*, a condition where the sufferer has difficulty pronouncing the *r* sound, which is perceived as closer to *w*.

78-80. **I praise the God Apollo...Zeus's bolt:** In Greek mythology, Apollo was known as the sun god and Zeus, the king of the gods, had dominion over the sky. His symbol was the thunderbolt (lightning). Bilgewater, while a brilliant strategist, was apparently not familiar with the attributes associated with Mediterranean deities and might well have benefited from an edition of Edith Hamilton's *Mythology: Timeless Tales of Gods and Heroes*—available for $9.95 at Barnes & Noble or wherever fine paperbacks are sold.

Dine thee not upon these courses?
How say you trampled by some horses?
Now here's a thought that's really heinous.
A shaft of steel shoved up his anus.
I've many more.
The next more ghastly than its antecedent.

KING MILHOUS
But hold, dear Duke.
We needn't move in haste to waste this wascal...rascal,
Lest our foes take pause and verily surmise
That his demise would be our cause.

BILGEWATER
Quite right, your mighty Majesty.
Though, distrust of thee
Would sway to sounds of sympathy
Should it be known this precious prince of yours
Were found to fall on foreign shores.
Of course! Such delicious deviltry.
Dare I use the word genius?
Nay, modesty forbids. O very well, "genius."
I praise the god Apollo for this spike of lightening
That so brightly doth display so salient a solution.

KING MILHOUS
'Twould be Zeus's bolt
But yet to matter. Come you dolt,
Spit forth thy thoughts as strumpets spit their spunk.

BILGEWATER
My cunning scheme is doubly pleasant
Since it provides the slaying of two pheasant
With one sole rock.
Enroll young Hameo upon a dicey mission
Assessing the condition and position
Of the forces of thy fiendish foe King Bolingbras.
Sans finesse for espionage, he'll plunge into their hands.
And Bolingbras is known throughout all lands
For his appalling penchant for gut-wrenching death
To those who would depose him.

101-2. **Thy father...rancid smell:** This is an homage to a line from *Monty Python and the Holy Grail* (1975) in which a French soldier taunts King Arthur by saying "your father was a hamster and your mother smelled of elderberries." I guess if you're going to steal, steal from the best.

Flourish: Hameo's trumpet flourish is from *Wind Beneath My Wings*—Bette Midler (1988). However, I think a fun alternative would be the theme from *Superman* (1978). Hameo could enjoy this heroic entrance and strike various Man of Steel poses. He could then tip the trumpeter and say, "Go get yourself something nice."

And thus, with righteous rage,
'Tis time to trash your truce
And wage the war you've waited for 95
With Hameo as your excuse.
'Twill not be sport but noble duty
To fight this foe and kick his booty.

KING MILHOUS
What an inspired conspiracy.
Thou art truly demon spawned from hell. 100
Thy father was a goblin;
Thy mother had a rancid smell.

BILGEWATER
Oh, you're not so good yourself.

Enter a Servant with trumpet.

SERVANT
    [*Flourish: "Did you ever know that you're my hero?"*]
Prince Hameo to see you, sire.

        Enter Hameo.   [*Exit the Servant.*]

KING MILHOUS (*to Bilgewater.*)
Let's put this plan upon its legs and set it running. 105
(*To Hameo*) Hameo, my brother's son.
How now? What news? What sport? What fun?

HAMEO
A word with you and you alone.

BILGEWATER
I take my leave. Away with me.
From thee, your excellency, I exeunt. 110
Farewell, auf Wiedersehen, good night.
Parting is such...

KING MILHOUS
GET OUT!!!!

                [*Exit Bilgewater.*]

Now Hameo, be kind enough to speak thy mind.

HAMEO
As thou do knowest well, 115
The passage of my father is no further from my heart

126. **'Tis mystery, enigma swaddled:** In 1939, with regard to the actions of Russia, Winston Churchill was quoted as saying "It is a riddle, wrapped in a mystery, inside an enigma." There are some historians that believe he further stated it was "cocooned in a conundrum, enveloped by a puzzle, encased in a burrito and stuffed into a turducken"—although to date, this extended version of the quote remains unverified.

142. **place a choly on my melon:** This is a fancy way saying that Milhous is experiencing melancholy or sadness at the passing of his brother.

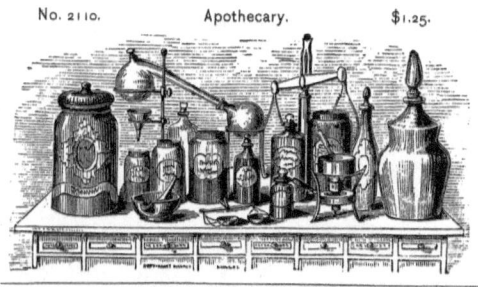

>   Than on the day he did depart from us
>   And slip his earthly mooring
>   To chart a course towards eternity.
>   What churns in me is that I do not know; 120
>   Was he called up by a higher force
>   Or pushed up from below?
>   Please tell me of the circumstance.
>   You knew him well. You wear his pants.

KING MILHOUS
>   In truth, I know no more than thee. 125
>   'Tis mystery, enigma swaddled.
>   The apothecary tried bottle after bottle
>   Of tinctures and a wealth of herbs
>   That do deny disease and fortify the health,
>   Alas to no avail. The ailment seized and 130
>   Throttled out his spark.
>   And when we spoke, this alchemist proclaimed
>   The culprit for his body's failure
>   Entered through his genitalia.
>   So heed me, son: 135
>   One must take care where plants one's post.
>   Protect that well which men prize most.
>   Aside from this I know not further
>   'Bout the gist of father's mur...uh...death.
>   I, too, feel thy pain. Forget not thy begetter 140
>   Was a brother dear to me. And just as thee,
>   His passage placed a choly on my melon.

HAMEO
>   I thank thee uncle for thy candor.
>   Think not it my intent to slander thee
>   With accusation. Bereavement's left my mind 145
>   Devoid of reason and of courtesy.

KING MILHOUS
>   Nephew, feel not at fault. There are few
>   Who curb their temperament in times of woe.
>   But even so, thou must endeavor to assuage
>   The nature of thy birth. Regretfully, I must unearth 150

154. **William came unhinged...picnic:** William Inge authored the play *Picnic* (1953), which garnered him the Pulitzer Prize for Drama.

160-61. **chowder of calamity...crackers:** Who doesn't enjoy a nice bowl of clam chowder, especially when it's accompanied by some fresh Saltines.

167-68. **libido's satisfaction well in hand:** What jerk really needs an explanation for this?

The buried truth as to the madness
That gallops through thy lineage.
Remember I when thy dear cousin
William came unhinged—it was no picnic.
And now it comes to me   155
Ye do address the midnight air.
And thus methinks these cousins do compare
In their insanity. I prithee,
Relinquish thy despondency and be thee not a pouter.
Calmly swallow down the chowder of calamity,   160
Lest people call thee crackers.

HAMEO
  There's wisdom in thy words.
  Yet I know not the way
  To slay these demons that possess me.

KING MILHOUS
  I have just the thing. I shall send thee abroad.   165

HAMEO
  Much thanks, uncle, but I'd rather choice mine own.

KING MILHOUS
  No doubt thou hast thy libido's
  Satisfaction well in hand.
  But when I spake "abroad"
  Know thee meant I some foreign land.   170
  Bolingbras, my nemesis, is rumbling at my borders,
  Therefore accept my order
  To infiltrate his ranks, discern his intent,
  And then return and let us know
  Upon what plans this devil's bent.   175
  And take thy friend Lymetrius with thee, if it so please.
  And be assured that this heroic jaunt
  Will jolt thee from thy spell.
  And we shall all rejoice in thy recovery
  When thou returnst to me all dressed in valor.   180

HAMEO
  I'll not have this fabric.
  It flatters me not and 'tis impossible to clean.

184. **A head as hollow...Yorick:** This refers to the skull of a dead court jester from Shakespeare's *Hamlet*. I, too, consider myself to be "a man of infinite jest" but most find the hollowness of my head a more prominent attribute.

188. **boldly go upon this enterprise:** Many will no doubt be familiar with this reference to the 1960s television classic *Star Trek* whose tag line was "to boldly go where no man has gone before"—and knows that this *going* occurred aboard the starship Enterprise. Of course, if you're nerdy enough to have picked up a Shakespeare parody written in iambic pentameter, chances are you knew that already—as well as what Smeagol's "precious" is, who's the father of Kal-El and how many parsecs Han needed to make the Kessel Run. Live long and prosper!

195. **bones be grist for this Milhous:** referencing the expression "grist for the mill."

1.4 Thelonious, at the behest of Queen Patsy, gives Hameo and his son, Lymetrius, his sage yet befuddled advice before the two friends begin their dangerous quest.

KING MILHOUS
Valor not velour. I speak to thee in language metaphoric.
(*Aside.*) A head as hollow I've not seen since Yorick.

HAMEO
Perchance a change of atmosphere wouldst do me well. 185
I shall take my leave of thee and tell my mother,
Though her fears bring sorrow's flood unto her eyes,
And with first light of morrow
Boldly go upon this enterprise.

[*O.S. opening of Star Trek Theme is sung.*]

Father? Daddy? [*Exit Hameo.*] 190

KING MILHOUS
The die is cast. It has begun.
I've freed me from the father,
Now I circumvent the son.
Yea, ye may groan and hiss and call me louse.
Still his bones be grist for this Milhous. [*Exit.*] 195

1.4 *Enter Thelonious with his stuffed dog, Lobster.*

THELONIOUS
What a beautiful summer's day. Why yes, Lobster.
It is more temperate and more sweet than yesterday.
But who knows what tomorrow will bring?
And tomorrow and tomorrow. Shall we play?
Here Lobster. Here Boy. Come to Daddy. 5
Come to Daddy. Stay. Good Boy. Good Boy.
Now, fetch the stick. Come on. Fetch the stick!
Ah, thou art a wise old dog, as am I.
Conserve thy strength for whenst it's needed most.
Come, give Daddy a big kiss. Come on. Come on. 10
That's right. That's right.

Enter Lymetrius.

LYMETRIUS
Father.

THELONIOUS
Look you, Lobster, who hath come.
My favorite son, Lymetrius.

Thelonious: This character is an analogue to Polonius in Shakespeare's *Hamlet*. His pet dog, which is a stuffed animal, is named Lobster in reference to Lance's dog in *Two Gentlemen of Verona* who is named Crab. Like Polonius to Laertes, Thelonious give his son, Lymetrius, a list of precepts or rules of moral conduct. Of course, in the case of Thelonious, these precepts make little sense as he is aged and senile.

LYMETRIUS
  Your only son, my father.

THELONIOUS
  And favorite son as well,
  Since I favor you over my other son—which I have not.

LYMETRIUS
  Yeah...anyway...
  My lord and friend Prince Hameo and I
  Must leave this day upon a perilous mission.
  He will be here anon. And for my sake,
  Conceal thee well the feature
  That thy mind's machine hath sprung a cog.
  Converse thee not with stufféd dog.

THELONIOUS
  'Tis true my dog is stuffed.
  But he has a weight condition.
  Should I then cease to speak to thee
  Should you put on a few?
  And why will Hameo meet us here a nun?
  He is neither woman nor religious.

Enter Hameo.

HAMEO
  Lymetrius, I give thee mine embrace.

LYMETRIUS
  I have received thy message and am at the ready.

HAMEO
  Fear not Thelonious,
  I will return thy son to thee unharmed.

THELONIOUS
  Well, better without arms than not at all I always say.

HAMEO
  No, no. His arms will be alright.

THELONIOUS
  And nothing on the left?

Flourish: This trumpet flourish relates to the famous Al Jolson song, "My Mammy" (1921). Please do not research this song as you may discover that Jolson sang this song while in blackface. The tune of the lyric "I'd walk a million miles for one of your smiles" is played as Hameo's own mother, Queen Patsy, enters.

Queen Patsy: The character, wife to King Milhous, is named for Pat Nixon, wife of Richard Milhous Nixon.

46. **All the world's a stage:** from Shakespeare's *As You Like It*. I'll go with doggy style...but that's just me.

HAMEO
  No, there'll be one on each side.

THELONIOUS
  Good! Two arms, one on each side. I like it.
  Now, what's all this 'bout you becoming a nun?

HAMEO (*to Lymetrius.*)
  Shall we go?

> *Enter a Servant with trumpet.*
>
> [*Flourish: "I'd walk a million miles
> for one of your smiles."*]
>
> *Enter Queen Patsy.*

HAMEO
  Mammy!

QUEEN PATSY
  Hameo, wert thou to leave without a hug maternal?

HAMEO
  Mother dear, there's nothing more infernal
  Than the eternal role of child.

QUEEN PATSY
  Well my son, all the world's a stage
  And irregardless of your whereabouts or age
  So long as thou do prance upon this earthly proscenium
  That part you'll play and my boy you'll be.

THELONIOUS
  Dear lady, thou shouldst be queenly proud
  Not motherly concerned.

QUEEN PATSY
  Good Thelonious,
  Dissuade them from this act of madness.

THELONIOUS
  Alas 'twould be to no avail.
  Young men must sail upon adventure's seas
  And wage the wars that so displease their elders.
  'Twas the same when I was spry.

62. **'Tis the thing...against the thigh:** That's right. It's a dick joke. You got a problem with that?

73. **Neither borrow nor lend a bee...sting you:** The original line from *Hamlet* is "Neither a borrower nor a lender be"—especially if the currency of exchange is insects. They really have very little value anyway.

75-76. **Thou may leadeth a horse...OK:** from the adage, "You can lead a horse to water but you can't make him drink"—nor should you. Alcohol addiction is a horrible thing. Just let that old nag finish its 12 Hoof Program in peace. It's hard enough pulling a wagon without falling off it too.

86-87. **To err is human...another planet is not:** from the adage: "To err is human; to forgive, divine." (But there's nothing divine about having three heads and coming from another planet. These creatures are green; they're slimy, and from what I hear, lousy tippers!)

Manhood is a thing that must be earned,
Though many have been urned in pursuit of it.
Know thou art a man and then all else be damned. 60
It puts the swagger in the step, the glisten in the eye.
'Tis the thing that beats within the bosom
Not that which slaps against the thigh.

QUEEN PATSY
Good Thelonious, let not them leave
'Fore thou doth pass along thy sage advice. 65

THELONIOUS
I have lived many moons, my son.
The wisdom of the world resides
Beneath this wrinkle brow.
So take to heart what I impart to thee this day.
These precepts will stead you in good stand. 70
Learn them well and keep them
At the ready, close at hand.
Neither borrow nor lend a bee, for it will sting you.
It would be rash to wipe thyself with three leafed plants.
Thou may leadeth a horse to water, 75
But if you don't want to it's OK.
Thou gets what thou pays for,
Unless you pay too much, then you're screwed;
But keep the receipt 'cause it's good for tax purposes.
Look before you leap; but if you leap off a mountain 80
All the looking in the world is not going to help you.
If you cannot see the forest for the trees
Find thee an optometrist.
The more things change, the more confused I get.
No pain...is a good thing. 85
To err is human,
To have three heads and come from another planet is not.
Honesty is the best policy, if you're an idiot.
The grass is always greener...I don't know why.
What's with that grass, anyway? 90
Two heads are better than one;
But if you have three heads and come from another planet
You're still not human—nothing's changed about that.

99. **Every dog...shit outta luck:** You know who's really fucked though? — turtles. Just think about it. They gotta carry this big shell around everywhere they go. Then some douchey kid is going to find one and start hitting it with a stick. What a nightmare.

1.5 While on their journey to the castle of Bolingbras, Hameo and Lymetrius encounter the Two and a Half Witches, a coven of mystics that dwell in the forest. They are so named since one of the witches provided a fortune that was so displeasing, her legs were cut off and she is forced to roll about on a small dolly. Hameo and Lymetrius are given cryptic prognostications about the women each will fall in love with and Hameo's future as a king. The two are then directed to the inn of Fatstaff, where they will find accommodation for the night.

7-9. **We have no date...rosy felt:** One of my favorite little bits of wordplay. One of our greatest presidents, Franklin Delano Roosevelt, in his first inaugural address proclaimed "The only thing we have to fear, is fear itself" and after the Japanese attacked Pearl Harbor, that December 7th 1941, would be "a date that will live in infamy."

If it ain't broke, try to borrow some money off it.
Necessity is the mother of invention. 95
The father could be either inspiration or ingenuity.
We don't know. I'm telling ya
That necessity is a fuckin' whore.
Every dog has his day. Cats are shit outta luck.
A friend in need is a real pain in the ass. 100
The early bird catches the worm. Well, whoop-de-doo!
Let 'em have all the goddamn worms
As far as I'm concerned.
The pen is mightier than the sword;
But if someone attacks you with a sword, 105
Drop the fuckin' pen and run.

LYMETRIUS
Indeed, we shall heed
All we've heard from you, dear dad.

HAMEO
And now we must away.
Though 'tis apparent our parents wish it were not so. 110
Whether live or die we do not know,
But know we well the answer lies at Bolingbras's
And so, in gear, let's put our asses. [*Exeunt.*]

1.5   *Enter Hameo and Lymetrius.*

LYMETRIUS
O, Hameo, this fiendish forest grows foreboding.
The trees have eyes, the rocks have teeth
And the leaves have a decidedly bad case of halitosis.
O, trusty shaft of steel, protect us well
From that which dwell within these barky walls. 5

HAMEO
Lymetrius, let not thine imagination best you.
We have no date with infamy.
You have nothing to fear but fear itself.

LYMETRIUS
Frankly, fellow, no rosy felt remarks of thine
Can quell the neck raised hairs or spiny tingle 10
Born within this lair where hellish creatures mingle!

26-30. **We dwell in brush...God damn it:** Doesn't it really suck when you and a couple of your witch buddies gather around a pot to do some first-class sorcery, and your incantations, which always end in the word *three*—because there's, like, three of you—don't really work anymore because one of you got your legs chopped off and so you're not really three anymore and are actually only two and a half?...Doesn't that suck?

HAMEO
  I strike thee for thy sanity.
  Allow me now to slay these demons
  Which exist but in the matrix of thy mind.
  What horrid goblin lurks behind this tree? 15
  Nothing there but a wisp of air.
  Around this boulder broods a fire-breathing beast
  Bent on burning balls for brunch?
  A firefly is all I spy. And here,
  What terror treads behind this brush... 20

HALF WITCH
  Ow! Ya just kicked me in the pussy.

HAMEO
  Reveal thyself, concealéd devil
  Or taste my saber's sting.

Enter Two and a Half Witches.

HALF WITCH
  Though famished I, I wouldst decline this metal meal
  And thus reveal my malformed self and sisters. 25

ALL WITCHES
  We dwell in brush and bog and briar.
  We conjure round a cauldron's fire.
  And speak of that which we foresee.
  The weird and wondrous witches th...

HALF WITCH
  Two and a half. God damn it. 30

LYMETRIUS
  Hameo, I have heard said of such a
  Party of prognosticators rumbling round this nook.
  Yet, lest I was mistook, they numbered three.

FIRST WITCH
  And so did we, before a fiend was so distempered
  With the fate for him we prophesied, 35
  He drew an axe clear cross my sibling's thighs.

39. You're as cold as...my tit: from the expression, "cold as a witch's tit."— apparently, baby witches like their breast milk chilled.

44-47. Forsooth...say our sooth: A *soothsayer* is a person who can supposedly foretell the future. Of course, if you do too much soothsaying you can wind up with a soothache.

SECOND WITCH
  How could one do such a thing?

LYMETRIUS
  You've stumped me (as, obviously, he did she).

HALF WITCH
  Laugh it up, Lymetrius. You're as cold as...my tit.

LYMETRIUS
  Forgive me fractional enchantress.
  I shall pay for my impertinence.
  Here's half a crown for half a crone. OK?

HALF WITCH
  'Salright.

HAMEO
  Forsooth, if we have stumbled cross
  A fortune telling coven, would it not be wise,
  Before good-byes, to hear the truth
  And have these sayers say our sooth?

HALF WITCH
  He always talk like that?

LYMETRIUS
  Be haggard not, dear hags.
  My lord and I must travel far and wide.
  The roads we stride do crawl with pending peril.
  Speak you now for good or ill
  What will befall us and we shall be
  Forewarned, forearmed and forever in your debt.

FIRST WITCH
  We have conferred.
  And so we two and half a third
  Will grant thy wish.
  Now gather ye 'round our portentous pot
  And see thee well of what will be and what will not.

68. **Two and a half...%@*&#!:** Just in case you were wondering WTF "%@!*&#!" means, after much research, I was able to discover that this is an arcane 15th century term that loosely translated means *fucker*.

75. **Of courseress:** This is an homage to a lyric used in the Oscar winning song "Talk To The Animals" from the 1967 film, *Doctor Dolittle*—and if you think it's corny don't throw a Bricusse at me.

ALL WITCHES
> *Eye of dog and lizard's gonads.*
> *What awaits our wandering comrades?*
> *Rotting skunk and bat vampire.*
> *Bare the good and what is dire.*
> *Muskrat snot and wombat turd.*
> *Let be known what must be heard.*
> *Unearthly demons hear our plea.*
> *Speak unto we witches th...*

HALF WITCH
Two and a half. Mother %@*&#!

FIRST WITCH
Get over it.

SECOND WITCH
Ah, look thee well,
This hellish brew doth now congeal
And thus reveals a vision to mine eye.

HAMEO
This knowledge is the beverage for which I thirst.
Fill my cup, dear sorceress.

SECOND WITCH
Of courseress. But be not seething
Should I see things quite adverse.
For I am not the causer of the curse
But just the messenger.

HAMEO
I will remember, not dismember.

HALF WITCH
Promises, promises.

SECOND WITCH
> *Though destined are ye for a throne,*
> *Ne'er will thee call a kingdom home.*

HAMEO
A throne without a kingdom? How can this be?

85. **diabolic bisque:** a type of soup commonly made by witches, largely comprised of horseradish, jalapeños and chili peppers. (If you're not a fan of bland soups, it also comes in Cajun style.)

95. **Adventurus interuptus:** a Latin term which refers to one being in the midst of an exciting adventure and then deciding, at the last moment, to withdraw from that adventure and cum all over its tits.

SECOND WITCH
Oh, it be. Truth may be riddle but rarely missed
When brought forth from our diabolic bisque.

FIRST WITCH
And now our foreboding broth
Doth cough up yet another sight:

> *Lymetrius,*
> *Though search ye wide and far*
> *For love's embrace,*
> *Know thee that thy belovéd,*
> *Whose elusive scent thou chase,*
> *Be but beneath thy very nose.*

LYMETRIUS
So then this lady fair's already known to me?
Adventurus interuptus. My lord, please do forgive.
I now must homeward flee to sate my curiosity
And find this damsel dear now destined to be mine.

HAMEO
Lymetrius, I grasp thy need, for 'tis the norm
To wish to speed thyself toward love's embrace
And thus, behold thy fated female's fetching form.
Her moistened lips, her saintly face,
The thrill of rounding second base.
So well I do recall when love first bites
Her venom can cause quite a swelling
And thus, I understand your ardor.

LYMETRIUS
'Tis true, I'm getting ardor as we speak.

HAMEO
But thou hast waited all thine age
And wait thou must a while more.
Unto our king we're duty bound
Until our journey's end. Till then, my friend,
Forget the stir in heart and crotch
Awakened by this base beeotch.

121. **Hold on thar, Baba Lymey:** a reference to the 1959 TV cartoon, *The Quick Draw McGraw Show*. The titular character would utter this particular phrase to his chum and sidekick, Baba Louey.

122-24. **semi sis, demi-demoness:** These synonyms, along with the previously mentioned "half a crone" and "fractional enchantress," were all commonly used terms for a witch that has been cut in two.

LYMETRIUS
  I do repent, good sire,
  For thinking with the head that hangs below
  And not with that which sits much higher.   115
  When duty's done, from service I shall be discharged
  And then perhaps...by service.
  Let us make haste,
  Then all the sooner shall I taste
  Of this delightful dish.   120

HALF WITCH
  Hold on thar, Baba Lymey.

FIRST WITCH
  My semi sis hath yet another tale to tell.

HALF WITCH
  Little help?
                          [*The other witches help her
                                 to the cauldron's edge.*]

HAMEO
  Perhaps, dear demi-demoness, thou could confess,
  If seen within the depths of thine unsavory soup, 125
  Is yet another lass with whom I might be destined
  Soon to pass the time of day—or better still, the night?

HALF WITCH
  Let's take a looky-loo. Uh huh. Uh huh. Ohhhhhhhhh.

HAMEO
  Spill thy guts or I shall spill them in thy stead.

HALF WITCH
  Keep your shirt on. I'm workin' here: 130

      Some dames are nice and dainty.
      Some dames they likes to cuss.
      This dame's got class, a rack and an ass
      And pulchritudinous.
      But though this bonnie's beauty   135
      May put thee in a trance.
      Ye must know this, please don't be pissed,
      But she likes to wear the pants.

149. **shrewish girl:** a young woman who practices shrewdaism as well as subscribes to Shrewdeo-Christian beliefs.

153. **hermaphrodite:** Genitally speaking, one of the most popular of the Greek goddesses.

HAMEO
  O, cursed-blessed am I
  With this distemperate peach 140
  The fates have pitted me against.
  To know the one to bear mine heir,
  With whom I wished to wed
  Beneath the whippoorwill,
  Will whip me with her womb 145
  And make of marriage misery.
  Yet mother would be pleased.
  She e'er did wish of me to marry
  A nice shrewish girl.

LYMETRIUS
  Perhaps ye can interpret thus. 150
  Perhaps to wear the pants may mean not shrew.
  Perhaps, dear Aphrodite has in store for ye
  Something more...hermaphrodite.

HAMEO
  (*Drawing sword.*) Engage thy brain
  Before thou let such lyric tumble from thy lips, 155
  As indeed thy head may yet tumble from thy neck.
  Wert this interpretation to be so,
  I'd gladly now accept the wound
  And run upon thy sword
  Before consorting with the sort 160
  With both a wound and sword.

HALF WITCH
  That's so not PC, dude. Junk is junk.

LYMETRIUS
  Be not vexed by this, my mere conjecture.
  Upon review, betwixt the two perchance to be,
  I now, like ye, do feel much firmer 'tis the former. 165

HAMEO
  Alas, 'tis no one but a fool
  That craves to know in youth
  That which he shall know too well
  When temples grey and lip doth drool.

176. **Yippee, Yappee, Yahooey:** homage to the 1964 Hanna-Barbera animated series. (These three characters were bungling palace guards—quite apropos for this piece. After the series ended, each character went their separate ways and one went on to become the founder of a successful internet company.)

The fault lies square 'pon my trapezius.   170
And though perhaps we wish it thus,
These devilish drabs can ne'er revoke
This future lump 'pon which I choke.

LYMETRIUS
At least, my lord, thou can take consolation
In mine own good fortune.   175

HAMEO
Yippee, Yappee, Yahooey.
And now as sun is close to slumber
We should lumber through this lumber
Toward accommodation.

FIRST WITCH
There lies at forest's edge   180
An inn whose keeper's mirth
Is known to only be exceeded by his girth.
Speak unto old Fatstaff that we,
The woodland witches, sent ye thither
And he will give thee care for modest fare.   185

HAMEO
Much thanks to ye, dilapidated damsels.
Come Lymetrius.

ALL WITCHES
    Beelzebubs with breasts and nipple.
    We've shown to thee the future triple.

HAMEO
    By dabbling in demonic craft.   190
    Ye weathered witches two and a half.

HALF WITCH
Hey! That's a good one.
Quick, somebody write that down.

                                                        [*Exeunt.*]

1.6 Fatstaff and his barkeep discuss the dire consequences of his tax obligations when Hameo and Lymetrius arrive at his inn. While Hameo goes off to engage in a romp with two bar wenches, Fatstaff entices Lymetrius to try his hand at a game of chance—Shells and Pea. Before long, Lymetrius has lost all his money and a bag of gold that Hameo entrusted to him. He then agrees to borrow funds from Hemlock, a cannibalistic money lender, with the terms that he must return the funds with interest in two weeks or provide Hemlock with a pound of flesh. Lymetrius loses these funds to Fatstaff as well in a final round of Shells and Pea. Fearing Hameo's wrath and his debt to Hemlock, Lymetrius flees the inn just as Hameo returns from his encounter with the wenches. Hameo learns what has transpired in his absence and runs off to find Lymetrius as Fatstaff revels in his new found wealth.

1.6 *Enter Fatstaff, Barkeep, Hemlock and Bawdy Men.*

FIRST BAWDY MAN
>*We drink to men in days of old.*

BAWDY MEN
>*With a hey nonny-nonny and a ha cha cha.*

FIRST BAWDY MAN
>*They left their wives and their households.*

BAWDY MEN
>*With a hey nonny-nonny and a ha cha cha.*
>*All the day we'll merry merry be.*
>*All the day we'll merry merry be.*
>*All the day we'll merry merry be*
>*At night we'll go a-wenching.*

SECOND BAWDY MAN
>*They'd steal their bread and drink their fill.*

BAWDY MEN
>*With a hey nonny-nonny and a ha cha cha.*

SECOND BAWDY MAN
>*Then in your lap they'd get real ill.*

BAWDY MEN
>*With a hey nonny-nonny and a ha cha cha.*
>*All the day we'll merry merry be.*
>*All the day we'll merry merry be.*
>*All the day we'll merry merry be*
>*At night we'll go a-wenching.*

THIRD BAWDY MAN
>*They'd fight and kill and wield an axe.*

BAWDY MEN
>*With a hey nonny-nonny and a ha cha cha.*

THIRD BAWDY MAN
>*They'd chew on nails and then fart tacks.*

BAWDY MEN
>*With a hey nonny-nonny and a ha cha cha.*
>*All the day we'll merry merry be.*

36. **tarred and feathered:** a form of public torture and humiliation in which hot tar is poured or painted on the body and feathers are applied. (My guess is after applying scalding hot tar to someone's body, they didn't start screaming, "Please, please—no feathers!") **drawn and quartered:** In medieval times, those convicted of treason would be tied to a plank and drawn by horse to a place of execution. There they would be hanged (almost to the point of death) then emasculated, disemboweled, beheaded and quartered (chopped into four pieces). Sometimes they were eighthed or sixteenthed to help the local kids learn about fractions.

39. **Ps and Qs:** The expression "mind your Ps and Qs" has several possible origins and meanings including, leaning your alphabet properly; do not interchange Ps and Qs when typesetting; make sure to say "please and thank you"; don't drink too many pints and quarts at the bar. Anyway, for godsakes—be careful!

All the day we'll merry merry be.
All the day we'll merry merry be
At night we'll go a-wenching.

FOURTH BAWDY MAN
They'd skip and prance and dance and sing.
With a hey nonny...nonny...
[*Exit Fourth Bawdy Man in disgrace.*]

BARKEEP
Fatstaff a word with thee.

FATSTAFF
What ails the keeper of the ale this night?

BARKEEP
This morn his majesty's tax collector...

FATSTAFF
A royal pain in my assets.

BARKEEP
Didst report shouldst thou resort
To tarry further in the payment of thy tariff,
Tomorrow noon the noble sheriff
Will hither come to pluck thee out from thine inn
And thou shalt be beheaded, de-feeted,
Feathered, drawn, tarred and quartered...
But perhaps not in that order.

FATSTAFF
Where canst I come by such sum in such a time?
Dear gents, mind not thy Ps and Qs this night.
Drink ye well, have thy fill and pay in full.
Reacquaint thyselves with long forgotten chits
And settle up with coins of metals.
Would thee not a wench or two to while away the hour?

BAWDY MAN
My funds are tight and they are not.
No doubt a yank will dull the need
And leave me so much more for mead.
Yet mean I no offense unto thy sisters.

61-62. **phoenix rise...thine ash:** In Greek mythology, a phoenix is a long-lived bird that bursts into flame upon death and is reborn from its ashes.

70. **succor:** assistance and support in times of hardship and distress—and if given properly, you may cause even more hardship. (When providing succor, it is common courtesy to also play with the balls.)

FATSTAFF
  Repellent rogue! How dare thee think
  I'd offer up my sisters to the likes of thee.

WENCHES
  You tell 'em, cousin.

FATSTAFF
  Confound this congregation!
  These mongrels' meager means
  Will mean an end unto my life and livelihood.
  So be it then if it must be.
  Well after all, my 50 years is not piddling while.
  I should smile that my stein was filled so well,
  Not curse that it was only filled but half.
  Pour me now my last carafe
  And I'll imbibe my final quaff
  And quit this world in sweet inebriation.

          Enter Hameo and Lymetrius.

BARKEEP
  Fatstaff, thou may yet like the phoenix rise
  Just as thou hast kissed thine ash goodbye.

FATSTAFF
  Dear gentlemen. A hardy welcome unto ye!
  I greatly praise the divine design
  That hast brought ye to abide in my abode.

HAMEO
  Thou canst attribute our arrival
  More to devil than to deity.
  Those foul females two point five of forest lore
  Proposed that we might here secure
  Some succor for the night.

FATSTAFF
  Abigail! Eloise!
  The two best suckers throughout the land.
  Guaranteed to please the eye and gratify the gland.

HAMEO
  Meant I sanctuary not oral satisfaction.

79. **libation:** a drink

85. **royal charge:** a duty or task entrusted to someone by a sovereign. Usually, a royal charge comes with 1.5% cashback or mileage points.

87. **Press not I upon thy privacy:** It is always important to not press upon anyone's privacy without their express permission.

FATSTAFF
  And why not both, my lord? 75

HAMEO
  Uh, rest thee here, Lymetrius,
  And I shall see if there art quarters worth our coinage...
  Umm, for about an hour or two. Ladies?

  [Exeunt Hameo and the Wenches.]

FATSTAFF
  A fine libation for thee, noble gent,
  For which the only recompense will be 80
  To sit and babble the retelling of thy travels.

LYMETRIUS
  I bless thee for thy brew
  Yet ne'er canst I reveal to you my journey's gist.

FATSTAFF
  I comprehend thy need to classify.

LYMETRIUS
  Save only now to say I am upon a royal charge 85
  Of which I cannot speak.

FATSTAFF
  Press not I upon thy privacy.

LYMETRIUS
  In truth, the very future of our lives and land
  May well depends upon the swift completion
  Of the task at hand—whose nature may not pass my lips. 90

FATSTAFF
  But of course, my lord.

LYMETRIUS
  We're off to spy on Bolingbras.
  Curse thee and thy relentless inquisition.

FATSTAFF
  Kind sir, 'twould seem that
  Thy commission's made a tumult of thy soul. 95
  Might I propose a simple game of chance
  As fair distraction from thy pending action?

102. **shells and pea:** This is a game of chance in which the operator, in our case Fatstaff, places a pea beneath one of three coconuts. He then proceeds to move the coconuts in such a manner as to confuse the viewer as to the location of the coconut hiding the aforementioned pea. The player (also referred to as *the mark*, *chump* or *sucker*) bets as to which coconut contains the pea. He will almost invariably be wrong and lose his money. Sometime a shill (in this case the barkeep) is employed to pretend to lose an easy round of manipulation in order to convince the viewers that they could do better—encouraging them to play. This game is sometimes played with cards and in such case is called Three Card Monty, named after famous game show host Monty Hall, who used to humiliate contestants by forcing them to dress up in ridiculous outfits.

LYMETRIUS
  A game of chance?

FATSTAFF
  If thou should be a man of sport then surely
  You'll submit unto my meager merriment.   100
  A test of concentration, speed of eye and of thy wit.
  Behold, the shells and pea.

LYMETRIUS
  A demonstration, if you please.

FATSTAFF
  Pea, pea. Where for art thou, pea?
  Know not you and know not me.   105

BARKEEP
  'Tis lurking 'neath this nut. A weekly wage upon it.

FATSTAFF
  And may this week pass briskly
  For thee and thy empty stomach.
  Care thee thy luck to try, my lord?

LYMETRIUS
  No doubt I'll fair me better than a fool. Play on.   110

FATSTAFF
  Pea, pea. Where for art thou, pea?
  Know not you and know not me.

LYMETRIUS
  A hundred ducats I will wager sure as hell
  Beneath this shell doth hide thy shy legume.

FATSTAFF
  Alas, no speck of vegetation here, my dear kind sir.   115
  Yet with thy next attempt no doubt
  Thou shall make full redemption of thy loss
  And then my ill-got booty be the one to bear the cost.

LYMETRIUS
  But I've no tender to expend,
  Save that I carry for my master;   120

137. **Thy luck be not so ladylike:** This is a reference to the 1950 musical *Guys and Dolls*, featuring the song "Lucky Be a Lady."

138-41. **nothing but a tramp...it's oak:** another song reference, this from the 1937 Rogers and Hart musical *Babes in Arms*, featuring the hit song "The Lady Is a Tramp."

> This bag of gold, the loss of which
> Would spell disaster for our enterprise.

FATSTAFF
> And yet how pleased thy lord would be
> To find his wealth was made two-fold
> Wert thou so bold as to accrue 125
> This precious loot so eager to be yours.

LYMETRIUS
> Rack 'em fat man.

FATSTAFF
> Pea, pea. Where for art thou, pea?
> Blah, blah, blah. Blee, blee, blee.
> Choose thee now and choose thee well, my lord. 130
> Ah, yes. No doubt thy fortune rests beneath this shell.
> 'Tis true, perhaps thy riches here may dwell.
> Thy fortune there 'tis feasible but who can tell?

LYMETRIUS
> Arrest the wagging of thy lips,
> Lest thou dine on shells and pea and fists. 135
> (*He chooses and loses.*) Ahhhhh!

FATSTAFF
> Thy luck be not so ladylike this eve, my lord.
> To thee she's nothing but a tramp,
> Too hungry for dinner at eight.

LYMETRIUS
> I'm broke. 140

FATSTAFF
> But it's oak.

LYMETRIUS
> What say you?

FATSTAFF
> This board 'pon which thou rest thy brow
> Was hewn from oaken limbs.

154. **The fault lies not in my scars...shells:** a play on the line "The fault, dear Brutus, is not in our stars, but in ourselves," from Shakespeare's *Julius Caesar*.

165. **Art thou Equity eligible?:** The Actors Equity Association is the union for stage actors. If you meet the requirements to join the union, you are considered Equity eligible.

167. **Olivier:** refers to Sir Lawrence Olivier, who is considered one of the greatest actors of his generation. He also starred in and directed a film adaptation of *Hamlet* (1948) which won the Academy Award for Best Picture and for Best Actor in a Leading Role. He was, to date, the only actor to win the Oscar for a Shakespearean role and the first to have won directing himself—and he never let anyone forget it.

150. *Iulius Cæsar Veneris beneficio in Cometam mutatur*

LYMETRIUS
   I care not for thy table's chronicle 145
   But more the saving of my genitals
   Which Hameo will surely have
   Whenst he discovers I've bobbled his bankroll.

FATSTAFF
   'Tis a pity. I have seen too oft
   The scars of humble bearing 150
   Goad impoverished men to daring
   Well beyond their means,
   And thereby taking it in their ends.

LYMETRIUS
   The fault lies not in my scars, but in these shells.

FATSTAFF
   My lord, I take exception should thou now infer 155
   Deception's at the root of thy dilemma.
   Impeach thee not my just won fruits.
   Although thy luck thou may be down upon,
   My game is surely on the up and up.

LYMETRIUS
   No doubt with one more go, the winds of just reward 160
   Should blow more kindly in my favor
   And erase the foul flavor of my forfeiture.
   Indeed, the laws of equilibrium will trim my loss
   And fate restore my state of equity.

FATSTAFF
   Art thou Equity eligible? 165
   Methinks I'd judge thee not by thy performance.

LYMETRIUS
   Excuse me, Olivier.
   But wither shall I find a kind advance of funds
   So I might tempt redemption's
   Now become my chief conundrum. 170

HEMLOCK
   My aged ears are filled with waxy clutter
   Yet did I not hear someone utter something of a loan?

Hemlock: This character is based on the moneylender Shylock from Shakespeare's *The Merchant of Venice*. Personally, I'm not sure what Jews were doing in Venice in the 16th century, but based on the outcome of the play, some people weren't happy about it. Shylock, too, asks for a pound of flesh from a borrower if repayment was not made. Whether he intended to eat it is anyone's guess.

188. **APR:** annual percentage rate (Since anyone reading this is probably up to their eyeballs in debt, chances are you are familiar with the term—which, on average, is about 12.54%.)

189. **masticate:** to chew (Of course, if you masticate too much you may go blind.)

193-94. **people who eat people...world:** refers to the song, *People* made famous by Barbra Streisand.

203. **With fava beans and a nice chianti:** the food and beverage pairing preferred by the character of Hannibal Lecter when eating the liver of a census taker in the 1991 thriller, *Silence of the Lambs*.

Solanio. How now, Shylock! what news among the merchants?
Shylock. You know, none so well, none so well as you, of my daughter's flight.
Act III. Scene 1.

FATSTAFF
   My lord, I do beseech you. Borrow not from him.
   'Tis Hemlock, the moneylender,
   A known offender of all that's decent and humane.   175
   He has a great disdain for all mankind
   And yet this twisted soul doth deign to dine
   On human flesh—a pound of which he'll coax
   As your collateral for any loan.
   And should thee dare default,   180
   Then 16 ounce of thee shall be his own.

HEMLOCK
   What thou hast heard I don't deny.
   Indeed, I do devour the indebted,
   Feast on the defeated, gum the gamblers
   And gnaw upon the scofflaws—and what of it?   185
   The world's a finer place by far
   Without the ilk who try to bilk
   An honorable cannibal of his APR.
   Do not berate a man for that which he doth masticate.
   We've all our own peculiar tastes.   190
   Some folks like anchovies, some caviar,
   Some kids eat paste.
   I happen to eat people—and people who eat people
   Art the luckiest people in the world.
   I solely do consume that which hath been   195
   Freely proffered by the raiders of my coffers.
   My terms should cause no grave concern
   Should thou fulfill thine obligation
   In a fortnight's passing. But if thou cannot,
   Swear thee now beneath thy God   200
   And before this drunken crowd
   To visit at my summer shanty
   With fava beans and a nice chianti.

LYMETRIUS
   My luck thus far's so sublimely cursed,
   I do surmise the worst of my financial state   205
   Is now behind and cannot be resigned
   To see this fat buffalo wing his way to bliss

213. **Yadda, yadda, yadda:** another way of saying, "Long story, short" popularized on an episode of the hit television series *Seinfeld,* which was actually written by my cousin. (Even though she had a lot of connections in LA, she was never really willing to help me with my writing career but I'm not bitter about—no really, I'm not!)

214-15. **up the creek...sans propulsion:** Why say, "I'm up shit's creek without a paddle" when you can make it sound all fancy and such.

216-20. **a fortnight...two weeks:** A fortnight *is* two weeks—duh!

228-29. **by the picking...that way goes:** a play on the line, "by the pricking of my thumbs, something wicked this way comes," from Shakespeare's *Macbeth*.

THE INCANTATION.—(*See page 5.*)

And give a miss to this
My last occasion for salvation.
I shall accept thy terms and 2000 ducats. 210
And with this final try,
Right all that which hath gone awry.

FATSTAFF
(*Mixing the shells.*) Yadda, yadda, yadda.

LYMETRIUS
(*Loses again.*) O, Now am I truly up the creek
Replete with fecal matter sans propulsion. 215

HEMLOCK
Well dear sir, I'll see thee in a fortnight.

LYMETRIUS
To gather such a sum in such a time is nigh impossible.
I prithee for a slight protraction.

HEMLOCK
Very well, my tasty friend.
Two weeks—and not moment more. 220

LYMETRIUS
Thou art as fair as thou art an abomination
Deserving to be crushed beneath the heels of Satan.

HEMLOCK
Oh, let me go before I get all mushy.
And by the bye, when the time is nigh,
My abode's just up the boulevard. 225
All know the way that you might query
Or merely...follow thee the bones.

[*Exit Hemlock.*]

FATSTAFF
By the picking of my nose,
Something wicked that way goes.

LYMETRIUS
I must speed me hence and blaze a trail 230
Afore mine entrails serve as Hemlock's nutrient
Or worst still, find themselves

241. **tristful visage:** sad face (This comes from a line in Shakespeare's *Hamlet,* "Heaven's face doth glow o'er this solidity and compound mass with *tristful visage*, as against the doom...)

242. **dicer oaf...rhapsody of turds:** from a line in Shakespeare's *Hamlet,* "Such an act that blurs the grace and blush of modesty, calls virtue hypocrite, takes off the rose from the fair forehead of an innocent love and sets a blister there, makes marriage vows as false as *dicers' oaths*—o, such a deed as from the body of contraction plucks the very soul, and sweet religion makes a *rhapsody of words*!

245-46. **wrath doth wane...wax?:** To *wane* is to diminish in vigor or intensity and to *wax* is to become more so. The terms are used most commonly in reference to the brightness of the moon but are often confused for one another.

247. **Wane, wane...another day:** from a children's nursery rhyme involving *rain.*

Wound 'round my master's blade
For he didst bade me ward his wage.
 A duty I didst fluff 235
Whilst he didst dive amongst the muff.

HAMEO (*O.S.*)
 Lymetrius!

FATSTAFF
 Thy master prematurely came and now doth hither come.
 Whilst life still course in thee, depart the pub
 And flee the marketplace. 240

LYMETRIUS
 Yea, go I now with tristful visage in disgrace;
 All due to you, you dicer oaf and your rhapsody of turds.
 This folly doth my conscience tax
 And ne'er dare I return again
 Until my master's wrath doth wane. 245
 Or is it wax?

FATSTAFF
 Wane, wane! Now go away. Come again another day.

 [*Exit Lymetrius. Enter Hameo.*]

 How now, my lord? Didst thou find our chambers
 (Bed and maids') suitable for repose?

HAMEO
 Enough to curl one's toes. But where for art Lymetrius? 250

FATSTAFF
 Alas my lord, a band of gamblers didst,
 With trick, entreat your fellow traveler
 To dabble in a game of Shells and Pea.
 And when his fortunes ran asunder, thy fortune too,
 Engagéd for deliverance, was plundered, 255
 Flowing down the selfsame river
 To the pretty mouths of empty shells.
 But know thee well how fervently I pray
 He give this game a miss, yet he rebuffed
 And they didst from him take the piss. 260

267. **scared the chit out of him:** A chit is a voucher, typically recording a sum owed—although, it kinda sounds like the word *shit*, don't it?

269. **a teacup full of tempest:** from the idiom "A tempest in a teacup (or teapot)," meaning a small event that has been exaggerated out of proportion. (A similar idiom, "A kerfuffle in a Cuisinart" never really caught on. Also, there is a play by Shakespeare entitled *The Tempest*.)

270. **Much ado about nothing:** another Shakespeare play—as if you didn't know. Don't you like it when I talk down to you?

277. **I got your gist:** Please don't make me explain this. For further information, just google *Clinton, Monica Lewinsky, Blue Dress.*

HAMEO
And since I sense Lymetrius is not about,
This tale hath more to tell—so with it, out.

FATSTAFF
Forsooth; at last resort didst thy companion consort
With a man-eating fiend who proffered a loan
That must be paid, if not in coin, then flesh and bone.
When all was lost, he fled his debt for life's desire
And from thine ire, which scared the chit out of him.

HAMEO
Oh foolish youth that flee from
But a teacup full of tempest.

FATSTAFF
Forsooth, my lord. Much ado about nothing.

HAMEO
Though peeved by his misplay, he should know still
I love him well—but not in that way.
And so must I o'ertake Lymetrius. (*to the maids.*)
Though rather would I stick and ride out the night
Betwixt your pillows, if you get my gist and thrust.

ELOISE
Oh, we got your thrust alright.

ABIGAIL
I got your gist all over me blouse.
That's not gonna come out.

HAMEO
And so away with me, good people
As I go not gentle into that good night.
Rage, rage...

FATSTAFF
Uh...wrong poet, my lord.

HAMEO
Well then good night.
Parting is such sweet sorrow. Happy?

[Exit Hameo.]

285. **Ale's well that ends well:** a play on *All's Well That Ends Well*—another of Shakespeare's works.

288-9. **hickey...taxman cometh:** This refers to the Eugene O'Neill play *The Iceman Cometh*, in which the lead characters name is Hickey. It in no way refers to the Ryan O'Neal movie *So Fine* (1981) in which his "haughty haunch" is exposed through a pair of assless jeans. Warning—once this is seen, it cannot be unseen.

291. **the avenue of ease:** otherwise known as Easy Street.

292-3. **A wealthy man...daiddle dum:** This refers to the song "If I Were a Rich Man" from the 1964 musical *Fiddler on the Roof*. This is something I have no fear of becoming from the publication of this play.

BARKEEP
   Fatstaff, a toast to thee. Ale's well that ends well.   285
   Mammom's smirk didst jerk thee clear of debtors' prison.
   No longer need you genuflect or kneel
   Or give his haughty haunch a hickey
   Whenst the taxman cometh.

FATSTAFF
   My mirthful mixologist,   290
   Reside now I upon the avenue of ease.
   A wealthy man with a princely sum.
   Daidle deddle daidle digga digga deddle daiddle dum.

                                                      [Exeunt.]

A Bard's Day's Night
('s Dream)

ACT II

2.1 Julinia, the daughter of King Bolingbras, and her maid, Hippopotima, wander in the woods to enjoy a summer picnic. While Julinia goes off to relieve herself, Hippopotima laments her overweight condition as an impediment to finding love. She is about kill herself when Schmuck appears, stopping her with a magic flourish. He then enchants both her and Lymetrius (who is asleep beneath a bush) such that the first thing they see upon awakening they will fall in love with—assuming it will be each other. Hippopotima awakens to find Lymetrius asleep and falls madly in love with him, but is forced to run off at Julinia's beck and call.

22-23. **velvet fog...melt (or maketh:** reference to famous '50s jazz singer Mel Torme, whose voice was so smooth he was nicknamed *The Velvet Fog.*

ACT II

2.1   *Enter Julinia and her maid, Hippopotima.*
            Lymetrius sleeps unseen beneath a shrub.

JULINIA
  Oh, on such a summer's day as this
  Who can say what escapades may befall
  Two wanderers in the wood.

HIPPOPOTIMA
  My lady, prithee, rest awhile.
  To scamper so 'tis not convention   5
  For one so hindered by dimensions.
  And know thee well that
  Promiséd have I unto Lord Bolingbras,
  That by my watchful eye, his darling daughter
  Wouldst fall not prey to menacing marauders.   10

JULINIA
  Fear not, Hippopotima.
  For it is said that here enchanters dwell
  And favor well warmhearted souls
  In search of love and love's requite.
  Ne'er wouldst permitted be, harm to thou or me   15
  Or any such as we within their oversight.
  Perchance the magic of these parts
  Will quell the yearning of our hearts
  By sending forth, as we meander,
  Worthy men with whom we may philander.   20

HIPPOPOTIMA
  I wish it so, but for the sake of thee, Julinia.
  No mystic mist or velvet fog would melt
  (Or maketh less so hard)
  The hearts of men who scrutinize
  My double chin or thunder thighs.   25

JULINIA
  My dearest maid, why speaketh so with doubt and gloom?

HIPPOPOTIMA
  My rump could fill a rumpus room. 'Tis true,
  I've heard it said that I am likened to a whale—
  Which causéd me to wail indeed upon report of it.

44. **the stamina of Pheidippides:** a famed Athenian runner employed to warn Greeks of a Persian invasion.

45. **travel on from Marathon:** a play on the lyric "I'll travel on to Avalon" from the 1920 Al Jolson song.

47-48. **saturnine...tightish or loosish:** a play on the characters Saturninus (also referred to as Saturnine), Titus and Lucius in the Shakespeare play *Titus Andronicus*.

56. **You'll hear the belly's answer:** a line from the Shakespeare play *Coriolanus*.

Two score live I (and yet to score). 30
Oh the irony to be Moby yet ne'er know
The urgent sting of love's harpoon.
Upon the sea of love
No seaman yet lay anchor at my port.
They do prefer a much more dainty dish 35
And ne'er wouldst they give chase
To such a monstrous fish.

JULINIA

Hippopotima, do not blubber so.
Though it is not in the nature of our sex to do't,
Thou must give chase of man. 40
Lest thou be chaste anon.

HIPPOPOTIMA

Nay, my pursuit would give to even he
Of weakened knee and sore achilles
The stamina of Pheidippides,
Who'd travel on from Marathon to the Acropolis 45
To avoid one so abominably abdominous.

JULINIA

My maid, be not so saturnine or stormy
Over whether thy skin be tightish or loosish.
Thou dost dine on thine own deprecation
And save a slice of sorrow for dessert. 50
Now tell me true, could there not be a gentleman who
Wouldst o'erlook thy modest imperfection,
Rather finding favor in that which ye perceives objection...
Able?

HIPPOPOTIMA

I'll not respond to thee, but listen well. 55
You'st hear the belly's answer. No!!!

JULINIA

Thy distempered belly hast now souréd mine own.
I will away to yonder bush awhile.
Rest here beneath these early morning skies.

62. **May I...soliloquize?:** What Hippopotima is requesting here is permission to perform what in the theatre is referred to as *a soliloquy*—the act of speaking one's thoughts aloud directly to the audience. Pretty much what I've been doing in these explanatory notes throughout this play so far. Of course, I didn't have to ask anyone's permission. I can just go on and on and on—and no one's going to stop me. That's one of the benefits of self-publishing. Of course, you can choose to stop reading these notes and just concentrate on the play if you'd like...or throw the thing in the garbage and demand your money back—good luck with that!

72. **Respectively, we do our duty:** another *doodie* joke (Let's face it—doodie is funny!)

81. **A Tom (or Harry Dick), a Joe:** Did you figure out meaning behind Harry Dick all by yourself? You're getting pretty good at this.

HIPPOPOTIMA
  My lady?

JULINIA
  Yes, Hippy?

HIPPOPOTIMA
  May I...soliloquize?

JULINIA (*soto voce.*)
  Of course! What do you think they're going to do?
  Sit around while I wipe my ass?
  And whatever you do, just keep it light, OK?
  I've got a good scene coming up later
  And I don't wanna lose them. (*robusto voce.*)
  And so, rest here beneath these early morning skies
  And think thee thoughts of gaiety and fun
  Whilst I do take a royal one.
                                         [*Exit Julinia.*]

HIPPOPOTIMA
  She must go and me decreed to wait.
  Respectively, we do our duty.
  She followeth her gut's incline, as I do mine,
  For where my gut proceeds
  E'er will myself be found behind.
  A prisoner of appetite and ne'er allowed to be petite
  For sweets entreat one weak of will
  And their allure be doubly so
  When void in heart (and down below).
  When shall I ever chance to know
  A Tom (or Harry Dick), a Joe,
  To charm and wrap his arms around my fleshy frame?
  (If arms of such a length be found for such a dame.)
  My mistress persists to say, with each and every day
  It's right I should think more of me.
  And that I do, for it is true,
  With every day and every bite there is yet more of me.
  In fact, enough for four of me.
  How easily for to advise? She of slender hip and thighs
  Ne'er grasp the fate of fattish folks.

92-118. **peachy...unto ye, I surf:** You might have noticed that Hippopotima's soliloquy is gently peppered with a veritable cornucopia of food puns. Bon appétit!

Her butt ne'er be the butt of jokes.
Nay, all is peachy for such a sweet tomato
Who needs not fish for condiments
Or curry flavor with the gents.
Her salad days are well at ham. 95
And me, to any male, I'd stake my clam.
Bread-shouldered or shrimpy, mox nix,
So long as he not quail or duck
Or chicken-out from my advance
Or hints of horizontal dance 100
With profferings of sausage from his pants—
Now that wouldst be the icing on the cake.
Fuck, I'm hungry!!
Forgive, for I meant fudge.
O, woe for me this drudgery; 105
To hide in layers adipose
The things within that matter most.
So if ye be allies, do sympathize,
And let thine eyes perchance to well en mass
For those like me, who all must 110
Drown their hells in Häagen-Dazs.
I am aghast that I should be
A gastronomic anomaly. I can stomach it no more,
So I shall soar forthwith from this sad height,
To mash this stuffed potato and let my gravy flow. 115
And so with one last dollop of great courage and resolve,
I bid a not so fond adieu unto this tragic turf,
Then set my sail, let loose a wail and unto ye, I surf.

Enter Schmuck who freezes
Hippopotima with a magic flourish.

SCHMUCK
Miss me? Or hast thy warm affection been rerouted?
I'll not pout, for I surmised a quandary of that size 120
Would justly generate some empathy,
But none-the-less, methought I'd intercede
And spare ye the full gravity.
And yet what have I for my sweat?
No accolades? No vast parades? 125

126. **Saved ye within time's nick:** referring to the idiom, "in the nick of time"—the last possible moment before something begins or ends (It was also the inspiration for my spec script, *The Nick of Time,* in which a forensic pathologist, Nicholas Movado, constructs a time machine and travels into the past to solve legendary cold cases. All the while, sexual tension mounts between Nick and his lovely assistant, Tuesday Longines. Will they or won't they?—tune in to find out!)

155. **I learned it from a Keebler elf:** Pucks and elves have shared both the forest and their knowledge of a wide assortment of spells, incantations, charms and other various forms of enchantment for millennia. The Keebler elves were renowned for specializing in pastry-based magic which was considered to be "uncommonly good."

157. **trippingly on the dung:** a play on a line in *Hamlet* in which the prince instructs his players to speak their lines in a nimble fashion or "trippingly on the tongue."

Saved ye did I within time's nick
And offeréd not even once a frickin' glass of lemonade.
What's with you people? I could go and leave ye flat
And then this crush of audience would surely be just that.
Thinner than a whole-beef patty, 130
So give it up 'cause who's your daddy?
Oh flatter not, my friends.
I'm merely trolling for regard
Which comes quite hard for some,
OK, well then for me at least— 135
Being what I am, but half a man and half a beast.
If equal all, I'd now enthrall
With tales and dance and song,
But the laws of physics
May be flummoxed only for so long. 140
And thus, my puffy paralytic,
I do plump thy mass upon the moss
And with a fancy flourish bid
(When once more thou art cognitive)
Do not be fraught by grand depression; 145
Neither that, the cause of countless sighs
Which robs the soul of mirth,
Nor that, which thou didst just now make
So deep upon the earth—quake I to think of it.
So heed my incantation, which I strengthen apropos 150
With sprinklings of chocolate chips
And magic cookie dough.
And with such stout ingredients
This spell thou must obey.
(I learned it from a Keebler elf 155
Not too far down the way.)
Now who so lieth here, trippingly on the dung?
Why zounds, it's young Lymetrius!
(Should my surprise appear to be sincerity bereft,
The cause, my soul, I've seen it all 160
From right there upstage left.)
What freakish fate would bring these two so near?
It's queer to me, but no need to discuss.
If destiny decree it should be thus,

183. **deus ex machina:** a Latin phrase meaning "god from the machine"—a term coined from the conventions of Greek tragedy in which actors playing deities were mechanically raised or lowered onto the stage. The term has come to mean a plot device that solves an insoluble situation. (*Machina* is pronounced with the accent on the first syllable and a hard "c", but in this case, it should be spoken as a rhyme with the monologue's aforementioned female lady parts.)

185. **Rip Van Winkle:** a character in a Washington Irving short story who falls asleep and awakens 20 years later (This also happens quite often to audience members of this play.)

199-200. **golden slumber...and the beetles in his hair:** a reference to the song *Golden Slumbers* by The Beatles.

Would I not be obliged to play my hand
And be the card I am, the twine of hearts?
For starts, I'll plop him by this puddle, so.
And with a hoofful of my magic stuff,
Proclaim when next thine eyes do ope,
What first thou see, to thee, be dope.
For those colloquially impaired
Or who just don't get 'round too much,
That means he'll find it great and swell
And keen and fine and such.
And even more, he will adore until the end of days
The beauty he'll perceive in that upon what first he gaze.
My work is done so I shall run,
But when expected least,
Should merriment be wanting
Ye shall have your sexy beast.
For now, I bid farewell to ye of ballsack and vagina.
I'll be your man should the plot need a hand
Or a deus ex machina.

[Exit Schmuck.]

HIPPOPOTIMA
How odd to off and nod and know it not?
It seems I pulled a Rip Van Winkle
Whilst Jul pooped off to take a tinkle.
Well, let me rise out of this dirty ditch
And switch the foul remnants from my raiments.
Not wanting to invoke undue concern,
There is a man asleep upon the ground.
My whispering doth serve a double cause.
Firstly, as not to wake this weary soul,
And B, I cannot for the life of me recall,
As I am soon to faint from joy and fright,
And yes, the sudden onset of a slippery delight.
This man didst fall like manna from the skies,
As far as I surmise,
A gift from heaven faithfully implored.
And when he doth shake off his golden slumber,
And the beetles in his hair,
This gift shall be most thoroughly explored.

202-5. His form...and then we'll...: At this point, I found it difficult to find an appropriate word that rhymes with pluck, amok and buck. If you have any suggestions, do let me know.

2.2 Lymetrius awakens and sees the reflection of a protruding nostril hair from his nose in a small puddle, and entranced, immediately falls in love with it and merrily departs. When Hippopotima returns with her mistress and Lymetrius cannot be found, Julinia believes her to be deranged from lack of food. Yet upon Lymetrius's return and profession of love for his nostril hair, Julinia realizes it is he that is truly deranged and the three head back homeward where they can care for the deluded Lymetrius.

His form unto my heart strings pluck.
We'll drink and dance and run amok.
I'll tear the clothing from this buck
And pull him close and then we'll... 205

JULINIA
Hippy!!!!!

HIPPOPOTIMA
Reverus interuptus! You bade, my maid?

JULINIA
I did, indeed. Within my reach,
I have deflowered plant and shrub
Yet still do lack of foliage with which to end my rub. 210

HIPPOPOTIMA (*to Lymetrius.*)
I shall return, my love,
But now I give you leave,
As I must now give leaves unto my mistress.

[*Exit Hippopotima.*]

2.2   *A Rooster crows in the distance.*
Lymetrius awakens.

LYMETRIUS
Why is it that the cock is always
First to rise upon the morrow?
Were I not so weary, I'd sincerely choke the chicken
Till his head be spent and shriveléd.
But soft, this shining pool of morning dew 5
Unto me doth reflect a modest imperfection.
One nostril hair doth boldly dare protrude
Beyond a dark and crude olfactory lair.
Thus, with a yank, I'll aid in the escape.
And in the doing doth my mouth most surely gape 10
In purest admiration. The luster of this silken strand
Doth glisten so, enveloped in the sun's benign embrace.
And now I find within my heart a trace
Of what I dare not say, for it is saved for womenkind
And not for nostril hairs sublime. 15

24-25. **Should it be...gift within its mouth:** referring to the proverb, "Do not look a gift horse in the mouth." Also, *Nay* homonymically alludes to a horse's neigh.

29. **I'll tell two friends...and so on:** a tagline for a 1970s commercial for Fabergé Organic Shampoo.

Yet would it not be wrong for me to shun
The honeyed song of love so rarely sung
For fear the singer's avatar give rise to ridicule,
And then to leave me prone,
That from my very own be ostracized? 20
Then be it so, for love you know is wise,
And must we let unfettered run its course,
No matter what its chosen form or guise,
Should it be girl or snail or hair or horse.
Nay, 'tis wrong to look this gift within its mouth. 25
And so unto the world I will rejoice.
And like my vexsome friend, from break of day,
About my supple strand, I would crow on.
I'll tell two friends and they'll tell two and so on.
Because the gift of love is rare indeed, 30
'Tis but a fool to question or impede what feels so right.
And now that it has started,
Me and my hair shall surely ne'er be parted.

[Exit Lymetrius.]

Enter Julinia and Hippopotima.

HIPPOPOTIMA
  My lady, I do prithee, tarry not.
  Thou must bear witness to my wondrous find. 35

JULINIA
  O, Hippy, I am with thee just behind.
  Release my sleeve or damn thee to tarnation
  Before thou force my shoulder's subluxation.

HIPPOPOTIMA
  Forgive princess, if I forgot my place.
  'Tis surely my disgrace to have 40
  Exuberance my momentary master.

JULINIA
  Well, show me then where art thy handsome lad,
  Or give me leave to bandage my appendage.

HIPPOPOTIMA
  Why, he was here asleep beneath this shrub.

52-53. **Room of rubber...hatch of booby:** A *rubber room* is a padded cell for mental patients and a *booby hatch* is slang term for a mental institution. I have not experience either first hand but, no doubt, the day is coming.

59. **My brain is lost in sense and sensibility:** referring to the famed author of *Sense and Sensibility*, Jane Austen.

JULINIA
   O, Hippopotima I weep. 45
   For this hubbub is but delirium from lack of grub.
   Now eat thee well and have a sip of wine
   That presently thy faculty of mind may be restored.
   For I have seen it writ
   That sanity is prized above the ruby. 50
   And so, snap out of it
   Or thou will share a room of rubber
   Inst the hatch of booby.

Enter Lymetrius.

HIPPOPOTIMA
   Julinia, I need not convalesce.
   Although thou art distressed 55
   By what thou thinks a muddled mind,
   I shall assure to thee my brain is fine, not lost to lunacy.
   But were it lost then I would say to thee,
   My brain is lost in sense and sensibility.
   For all is clear and qualms are put to bed 60
   When romance comes to rear its lovely head.

LYMETRIUS
   Dear Ladies,

              [Julinia and Hippopotima scream.]

   I pray I have not startled thee.

HIPPOPOTIMA
   Julinia, why it is he, the bloke of which I spoke.

JULINIA
   Why sir, thou placed my heart within my mouth. 65
   I've ne'er obliged an organ of that size,
   Much less have need to swallow it with lunch.

LYMETRIUS
   A pardon to thee both a thousand-fold
   Wert I too bold yet soft in my approach.
   My manner was encroached this day by mirth; 70
   The moment I was wakened
   From my humble bed of earth, a vision I did spy

99-100. **winsome lass...you lose some:** *Winsome* means to be appealing in appearance—"wince some" and "win some" are plays on this term.

That so has alteréd my very soul,
All common cares and courtesies
Have fallen by the way. 75
Yea, even my belongings didst I leave
And only did just now perceive the lack,
Then hastefully returned to reacquire.

HIPPOPOTIMA
Dear sir, do tell of this beguiling sight
And let be known the thing that so enthralled 80
To render thine effects inconsequent.

LYMETRIUS
A beauty rare, none other could equate.
A form to cause one's spirit to elate.
A mode and grace that far outweighs the norm.
A temptress who wouldst take a heart by storm. 85
But why need be to hear of my report?
With thine own eyes behold what thou inquire.
For right before me lies my heart's desire.

HIPPOPOTIMA
A thousand kisses of my moistened lips
Could not give tongue to my new found delight. 90
Indeed, I do requite what thou confess.
Do name it now, the day on which we wed,
That I might share thy life, and too, thy bed.

LYMETRIUS
Dear maid, I am afraid thou art confused
And must abruptly disabuse thine err. 95
For 'tis another lady fair that doth
My strong affection hold within her grasp.
But 'tis no fault of thine, I do assure.
For know thee well, thou art a winsome lass.
(*Aside.*) Indeed, I wince some with my every glace. 100

HIPPOPOTIMA
Julinia, my love doth find me horrid.

JULINIA
No, no, dear Hippy. You win some, you lose some.

105-9. **Why thou didst say...why?:** If Hippopotima keeps telling Lymetrius he lied when she lied before him then she will never get laid.

HIPPOPOTIMA
  How couldst thou mock me so with thine advance?

LYMETRIUS
  I know of no advance and mock thee not.

HIPPOPOTIMA
  Why thou didst say thy love before thee lied.
  But thou didst lie before when that thou said.
  For I didst lie before thee whenst thou lied.
  And now thou say that I am not that love.
  And so thy love didst not before thee lie...before. Why?

LYMETRIUS
  No words that passed my lips were more so true.
  If thou dost lack the power to discern
  The subtleties of nature, fault me not.
  For yea, my love is here for all to see.
  Do gaze upon her now if thou should care.
  My perfect, lustrous, wondrous nostril hair.

JULINIA
  OK. We're outta here.

HIPPOPOTIMA
  Why no, my lady, I implore thee, no.
  'Twould be so low to leave one such as he,
  Devoid of reason and his sanity.
  No doubt 'twas these environs o'er the night
  That worked their twisted way upon his mind.
  And we should rest upon our Christian oaths
  And thus bestow not scorn but charity.
  We'll take him with and nurse his thoughts to clarity.

JULINIA
  Dear sir, do join us on our journey home.
  Thou must indeed of sustenance have need
  Which we would be most honored to provide
  Should thou concede our paths to coincide.

LYMETRIUS
  Thy generosity bespeaks a heart
  As warming as the hearth thou offeréd.

131. **Indeed, an offer made hearth-heartedly:** At times, Julinia can be rather hearth.

136. **And for my lady love, conditioner:** The key to any good relationship is to always make sure your lady is kept moist.

2.3 Hameo and Schmuck are en route to find Lymetrius as Schmuck recounts the tale of his enchantment and that of Hippopotima. Hameo reveals that he is aware of all that transpired, since he had read that part of the script. The two plan their journey to the castle of Bolingbras and Schmuck secures permission for his woodland friends (the audience) to join them on their quest.

---

1. **Quick! Somebody call the ASPCA!!:** The American Society for the Prevention of Cruelty to Animals (Schmuck would undoubtedly receive help from this organization since he is about five or six animals in one. However, it would probably have to be a long-distance call since these characters are somewhere in Europe at this time.)

6. **Atkins:** a ridiculous low-carb fad diet popular in the early 2000s (These days, everyone knows the Lemon Meringue Pie Diet is the only one that is scientifically proven to show results. The Macrobiotic Chocolate-Covered Kale Diet also looks promising.)

11. **Lymêtrius:** The Sheepyakgercoon mentioned in this passage is a truly majestic creature. If you should happen to have to good fortune of seeing one while out hunting in the forest, it may gambol over to you, grab the muzzle of your gun, place it against its forehead and beg you to pull the trigger.

JULINIA
  Indeed, an offer made hearth-heartedly.

LYMETRIUS
  Which I do now most humbly accept.
  Then off we go and from this forest flee.
  Some food and drink for me
  Will surely put things as they were.   135
  And for my lady love, conditioner.

                                              [*Exeunt.*]

2.3   *Enter Hameo and Schmuck.*

SCHMUCK
  Ahhh! Quick! Somebody call the ASPCA!!

HAMEO
  How dare thou ply enchantment 'pon the likes of me.
  Thy feeble dough presents as ineffectual
  When matchéd 'gainst my stout immunity.

SCHMUCK
  How can it be?   5

HAMEO
  I'm on Atkins. Now tell me straight
  What fate befell my mate, Lymetrius?

SCHMUCK
  My lord, though to thy will remain I bound and reverent,
  The man of whom thou speaks I do not know the referent.

HAMEO
  Then thou shalt die.   10

SCHMUCK
  Oh Lymetrius! Methought thou meant Lymêtrius,
  Which is not a man at all but 'tis my cousin—
  Half sheep, half yak, one quarter badger I would wager.
  And other bits as yet unknown.
  'Twas odd I thought you mentionéd of him,   15
  Whom I've not seen an age of coon within.
  In faith, he is one-eighth raccoon as I recall.
  I really must ring him up. You know it's been...

23. **cupidific:** acting in the manner of cupid or any other such winged bow-packing love baby.

41. **You carnally conglomerated klutz:** This is my homage to Dr. Smith (Jonathan Harris), the almighty alchemist of alliteration from the sensational '60s sci-fi series *Lost in Space*.

HAMEO
  LYMETRIUS!!!

SCHMUCK
  Oh yes, Lymetrius. Why yes, of course. 20
  Our last encounter was beside this shrub,
  Where like a weary woodland cub, he came to hibernate.
  Then play, did I, my cupidific role
  And tenderly did taint his humble sleep
  That in his waking he wouldst then behold 25
  A love as great as any yet foretold.
  And so my lord, do stow thy steel, I pray.
  I've done as thou hast bade
  And told thee all there is to tell on bended knee,
  Vis-a-vis this escapade... 30
  Uh, except the part about the fat chick.

HAMEO
  What?

SCHMUCK
  'Twould seem I came across a fleshy maid
  Whose form would ne'er to urge a man to chubby.
  And so didst I take pity on this tubby; 35
  Quelled her pangs
  By finding for her yin a worthy yang—
  Enchanting she as thy Lymetrius.
  It is my service if you will, if not my curse.
  My practice, that for which I'm well rehearsed. 40

HAMEO
  You carnally conglomerated klutz.
  Hadst thou conceived thy magic meddlings
  Could well unleash a havoc unforeseen?
  This maid of great expanse perchance may bade
  Her mistress over yonder making water, 45
  "Do come to see my splendid napping knight."
  And whilst distracted in her servitude,
  Complying with a wipe, Lymetrius
  Might waken by a pool with spellbound glance

51. **With the issue...muzzle choose to nuzzle:** As it has oft been said—"Fo' shizzle, my nizzle, you should never nuzzle with yo muzzle!

61-62. **the fabled road of yellow brick...brain:** You may contemplate the origin of this reference as you while away the hours consulting with the flowers.

63. **maleficent melange:** A little more alliteration for you—at no additional charge.

77. **you have meddled...Paddy Chayefsky**: refers to a line from the Oscar-winning film *Network* (1977), written by the aforementioned screenwriter.

80. **heretical hodgepodge:** Somebody stop me!

And like a fool, become improperly entranced. 50
Hence, with the issue of his very muzzle choose to nuzzle.
Then off he'd skips into the nearby wood.
Our ladies come but find not what they should
Till he returns for goods he'd left behind,
And so inclined, professing to the pair 55
His odd and glaringly uncanny fancy.
Finding him deranged,
Though she (like he) is similarly smote,
Our maid doth bade her mistress,
"Please pity this insanity." 60
And so the three stroll down the fabled road of
Yellow brick to get this broken bloke a brain.
What say you this, maleficent melange?

SCHMUCK
With all regard to thee that's due, my lord,
This portrait thou hast etched 65
Wouldst seem to most, at very least, far-fetched.
An odd synopsis showing that perchance
Thy mind's synapses all wert fired...
Without two weeks' notice.

HAMEO
Should what I quoth seem so far-fetched to thee? 70
Perhaps it is the truth that is far-flung from probability.
I must admit that normally,
Along thy view you'd find myself aligned.
Except I happen to take a peek at page 27 of the script
And that's exactly how it went down. 75

SCHMUCK
My lord,
You have meddled with the primal forces of nature!

HAMEO
And you've plagiarized Paddy Chayefsky.
So I guess we're both in hot water.
Now come, thou hairy little heretical hodgepodge. 80
We must give chase and thus o'ertake Lymetrius...

92. **woodland friends:** Wow, isn't it amazing? You, as the audience—or reader of this play—are actual *in the play itself.* And you didn't even have to audition, come to rehearsals, learn any lines or take any direction from me, which believe me, you really wouldn't have liked since I can be a real dick and very particular about performance and pacing and...well anyway, you're in the show. Unfortunately, I'm not going to be able to pay you anything for your performance 'cause you're not in the union, so just get out there and break a leg!

SCHMUCK
My lord.

HAMEO
And so restore my comrade to his quondam self...

SCHMUCK
My liege.

HAMEO
So that we two can quick conclude
Our promised quest, our royal charge.

SCHMUCK
My God! Thesbos is twirling in his tomb.

HAMEO
How darest thou to lash upon my bombast?

SCHMUCK
Oh sire, let this bygone be, for I do have a tiny inquiry.

HAMEO
What is it?

SCHMUCK (*referring to audience.*)
Uh...can they come too?

HAMEO
What? Thy little woodland friends? I would say not.

SCHMUCK
But sire, surely they must come.

HAMEO
And why is that?

SCHMUCK
Without them, this is just another rehearsal.

HAMEO
Oh, so be it—except for him. Slept through all of Act I
And thought I didn't notice? Oh yeah, I noticed.

SCHMUCK
But sire.

110. **And soft libations from the cola nut:** During intermission you might want to enjoy a nice, refreshing cold beverage. So walk right up to the concession stand and *Have a Coke and a Smile* or become part of *The Pepsi Generation*.

113. **Nor balms...solar savagery:** A lot of people think that two-time Academy Award winning actress Jodie Foster was the model for the original Coppertone ad depicting a dog pulling down the bathing suit of a young girl to reveal her untanned derrière. While Miss Foster did appear in television commercials for Coppertone in the 1960s, the artist responsible, Joyce Ballantyne Brand, used her daughter, Cheryl, as the model for this iconic ad. Just wanted to clear that up. By the way, could you imagine an ad running today showing a Cocker Spaniel pulling down a three-year old girl's bathing suit to show-off her bare white ass? People would completely lose their shit!

HAMEO
　Alright, him too.
　We'll need all the bluster we can muster.
　Prepare thee thine assemblage.
　We shall depart whenst the sun's life-giving rays
　Do brush the crest of yonder bluff.

SCHMUCK
　My lord?

HAMEO
　Give 'em 10.

[Exit Hameo.]

SCHMUCK
　Prepare thee well, compadres.
　The prince didst deign ye join in our crusade.
　The journey shall be long and arduous.
　Refresh thyselves with choice comestibles
　And soft libations from the cola nut.
　Then pack thee well thy satchels
　And disremember not thy dental bristles
　Nor balms to spare thy flesh of solar savagery.
　(I'd go with SPF 30 or above.)
　Now revel in thy respite,
　For we'll soon be 'pon the march,
　To find the prince's friend
　Then thwart an enemy who's arch.
　All plot twists will be straightened.
　Good and evil recompensed.
　How so you say? You'll know the way
　In 15 minutes hence.

Enter Hameo.

HAMEO
　I said 10, ya dumb puck!

SCHMUCK
　Well, ya know, give or take.

*[Hameo unsheathes his sword, chasing
　　Schmuck around the stage. Exeunt.]*

A Bard's Day's Night
('s Dream)

ACT III

3.1 Julinia, Hippopotima and Lymetrius arrive at the palace where Lymetrius is introduced to King Bolingbras, who reveals he is aware of the plan to spy on him. Hemlock appears and outs Lymetrius as one of these spies and he is thrown in the dungeon. Julinia vows to Hippopotima that she will find Lymetrius's friend Hameo to help save him by sneaking out of the palace dressed as a soldier.

---

12. **And in two dimensions cannot last:** Apparently, Schmuck is a creature that has the ability to exist in multiple dimensions and has powers and abilities far beyond those of mortal pucks. Is he faster than a speeding bullet? More powerful than a locomotive? Able to leap tall buildings in a single bound?—only time will tell.

ACT III

3.1   *Enter Schmuck. Guildencrantz and Rosenstern,*
          wearing moustaches, guard a palace gate.

SCHMUCK
  Well here you are.
  Although the same cannot be said of me.
  In actuality, I'm leagues away with master Hameo
  On route towards this locus.
  But with a bit of hocus-pocus   5
  I, your humble apparition,
  Thought it best to be your momentary chaperone,
  Affording continuity betwixt the acts.
  A friendly face to help ye bridge the gap.
  A kind remind for silencing the cellphones in your lap.   10
  What ho! Our ladies and demented gent come fro.
  And I in two dimensions cannot last for long, you know.
  And so on with the show,
  As I hightail it from these parts.
  I'll leave these three to babysit for ye   15
  With their dramatic arts.
  Were druthers mine, I'd split divine
  With smoky flames to make ye cough.
  But alas, our budget's tiny so in lieu I'll just walk off.

                                              [*Exit Schmuck.*]

          Enter Julinia, Hippopotima and Lymetrius.

JULINIA
  At long last home are we, as proiméd.   20

LYMETRIUS
  Nice digs, dear damsels, I must say to thee.
  Although, from what I see I fear
  Thou art no mere wood-wandering wench.

JULINIA
  Verily, I wouldst make known to thee
  My place as princess of these parts.   25
  Sprung off from good King Bolingbras.

LYMETRIUS
  Bolingbras?

29. **Yikes:** a term of astonishment and surprise; perhaps from yoicks, a call in foxhunting to encourage the hounds to pursue their prey. (May also relate to the experience of believing eggs to be hard-boiled but find upon cracking them that they are not, in which case one would exclaim in surprise, "Yokes!")

31. **Wthin the bosom of our hospitality:** Hippopotima's hospitality size is a DDD, but after a week of particularly heavy eating, can expand to as large as an F.

50. **Mostly:** I'm sure everyone can mostly remember Newt, the last survivor of the settlement on LV-426 in the film *Aliens*...mostly. If not, all I can say is "Game over, man! Game over"

51. **remember the porter:** a line from Shakespeare's *MacBeth*.

HIPPOPOTIMA
  My lord and master and the sire of my mistress.

LYMETRIUS
  Yikes! I fear I must dismiss myself, my lady.

HIPPOPOTIMA
  Why no, dear sir. Thou must take ease 30
  Within the bosom of our hospitality.

LYMETRIUS
  As ample and appealing as it be,
  My cherished friend and traveling chum
  Is plumb adrift within that sea of bark.
  I lost him on a lark and thus my spirit's run aground 35
  Till such a time as he is found.

JULINIA
  So shall he be.
  But firstly, let us dine on several courses
  And by all mean avail our vast resources.
  Thou wouldst not be so brusque to run and shun 40
  An audience with my papa and noble monarch.
  Come Hippy. We shall bring thee Bolingbras
  And food and drink. Fear not his reputation.
  He's but a lonely man whose love of company
  Is nigh on par with feeding foes their toes 45
  And genitalia. (*rings for servant.*)
  Wait here beside the guard, but a moment we shall be.
  I'm sure that meeting thee will be a thrill.
  He's known to take a shine to those he does not kill...
  Mostly. 50

  Enter a Servant, who take Hippopotima's picnic basket.

JULINIA
  Oh Lymetrius, remember the porter.

                    [*Exeunt Julinia and Hippopotima.*]

59. **Gilgamesh:** ruler of Uruk in southern Mesopotamia, 3rd millennium BCE.

60. **Mummenschanz:** a Swiss mask theater troupe, popular for its play with bizarre masks and form, light and shadow along with unusual choreography.

[Lymetrius searches for pocket change. Having none, he distracts the Servant and takes some change from his pocket, tips him with that, then pats his head à la Benny Hill while the theme music plays.]

[Exit the Servant.]

LYMETRIUS
Excuse me, aren't you...

GUILDENCRANTZ
No he's not.

LYMETRIUS
And you must be...

ROSENSTERN
Nor is that he. 55

LYMETRIUS
Rosenstern and Guildencrantz.
How come to pass ye guard the house of Bolingbras?

GUILDENCRANTZ
Methinks thou dost mistake us for some others.

ROSENSTERN
His mother gave to him the tag of Gilgamesh.

GUILDENCRANTZ
His moniker is rightly Mummenschanz. 60

ROSENSTERN
But thy befuddlement is justified.
Most guards possess an indistinguished puss, you see.

GUILDENCRANTZ
Most guards, moreless, are of the garden-type variety.

ROSENSTERN
'Tis true, we've been the guardin' type for most our lives.

GUILDENCRANTZ
As have our wives. 65

ROSENSTERN
We met on a double-date.

72-73. Truffles light as air...heaven in my mouth: a play on the lines "Trifles light as air are to the jealous confirmations strong as proofs of holy writ" from *Othello* and "Heaven in my mouth as if I did but only chew his name" from *Measure for Measure*.

[Flourish: the Darth Vader theme.]

GUILDENCRANTZ
  Oh Christ! Here he comes.

  Enter Julinia, Hippopotima, Bolingbras and a Servant.

JULINIA
  Dear father, may I make known our true companion.

BOLINGBRAS
  I'm told thy trek was toilsome indeed.
  The brief of which you'll soon proceed to tell.   70
  But presently, some simple fare to appetize.
  Truffles light as air.

LYMETRIUS
  Holy Writ. 'Tis heaven in my mouth.

BOLINGBRAS
  And now a toast.

JULINIA
  To what affair are we to raise a glass?   75

BOLINGBRAS
  The vanquishment of all our vile foes.
  This day didst bring report divulged to me,
  The spotting of that young Prince Hameo,
  And too his mate Lymetrius in tow.
  They garnered comfort at ol' Fatstaff's inn.   80
  And much to their chagrin, my sources say
  These bunglers are barreling this way
  In hopes that they'll undo me with a snoop.
  When they I apprehend their end shall be
  And endless sea of torment, pain, and misery.   85
  Their bones will snap and skin will scald
  And with the claws of beasts be mauled.
  And then, I'll pose for portraits
  Standing o'er their broken forms
  And send them 'round the land   90
  That all who gall me be forewarned.

94. **Geneva convention? Alright, no pictures:** Who can forget the heartwarming image of a female soldier giving a "thumbs up" next to the corpse of a tortured Abu Ghraib prisoner? Thanks to George Bush and Dick Cheney for showing the rest of the world what a good Christian country is all about.

102-6. **shown cunnery...No!:** Bond...James Bond.

SERVANT
  Sire.

BOLINGBRAS
  What is it? (*Servant whispers.*)
  Geneva convention? Alright, no pictures.
  So let us drink that all I say shall surly come to pass. 95
  And let us drink to you, sir. What's thy name?

            Enter Hemlock.

HEMLOCK
  Lymetrius!
                              [*Lymetrius faints.*]
  'Tis he for news of which thou paid so handsomely.
  Though ne'er would I surmise he had suffice
  The cunning to entice thy very own   100
  To pussyfoot him towards the throne.

BOLINGBRAS
  Indeed, this spy hath shown cunnery to be sure.
  (*To Servant.*) Rouse him!

SERVANT
  He has been shaken, my lord, but has not stirred.
  Shall I call the doctor?   105

BOLINGBRAS
  No! Guards!! Convey this slippery mole
  Down to his murky dungeon hole.

HEMLOCK
  My lord, this spy hath with his inky flesh
  Collateralized against his debt to me.
  I humbly ask that once you've had your way   110
  I may collect the dermis that is due.

BOLINGBRAS
  When I am through the offal shall be yours.

HEMLOCK
  Then off I'll go. Ladies.

                              [*Exit Hemlock.*]

122. **Not in 1512 AD you're not:** The 16th Century was actually a wonderful era for women's rights. Women of this time had the right to not be burdened with being able to vote or own property nor were they subject to the laborious task of attending school or choosing a husband. You go, ladies!

JULINIA
  But father, he is our friend to which we've made
  A pledge of warm reception and our hospice.   115

BOLINGBRAS
  Thou shouldst take greater care concerning whom thou
  Nestles neath thy wing, my budding chick.

JULINIA
  My father, do not daub me with the epithet of child;
  For I am full-blown woman through and though,
  With equal wit and wisdom to a man,   120
  And right to do and say as I see fit.

BOLINGBRAS
  Not in 1512 AD you're not.
  Take him away, then loose a legion for this Hameo.

                              [*Exeunt Guildencrantz, Rosenstern
                                            and Lymetrius.*]

  You muse that thou art every inch a man
  And yet the most important inches thou dost lack.   125
  You both are grounded to these grounds till I see fit,
  For I am King and you are nought and that's the shit.

                                            [*Exit Bolingbras.*]

HIPPOPOTIMA
  Julinia, I beg of thee,
  Let not my sweetie languish in the soup.
  Do curse me if with thee I must talk turkey,   130
  But I care not if he be sweet and sour
  Or at him should our lord be royally pilaffed.
  For he's my love; unless we save his bacon I'll go nuts.
  Fuck, I'm hungry.

JULINIA
  Dear Hippopotima, fear not to speak thy mind   135
  For I, as you, am womankind.
  And being such, have slight regard
  For reason or its rhyme.
  And should our whims and fancies
  Trigger chaos to ensue   140

150. **on the lamb:** The phrase "on the lam" comes from the word *lambaste*; to beat. It came into usage by echoing another slang term, "beat it"—meaning to run away or beat the road with your feet. Of course, if you are "on the *lamb*" it would be best to just pull out and *beat it* instead.

162. **No puny dictums of a man:** A man should never be judged on the size of his dictum but rather the girth of his edict and the motion of his mandate.

    Or governance should crumble
    Or should war erupt anew,
    These matters matter lightly
    For the likes of me and you;
    Providing love resides within our hearts 145
    And 'pon our feet a fashionable shoe.
    Now to the cause of thy Lymetrius.
    Much further we shall get with the abetting
    Of his dear friend, Hameo.

HIPPOPOTIMA
    But he is in the wood and on the lamb. Ooh, sorry. 150

JULINIA
    Then quickly I must go to search him out.

HIPPOPOTIMA
    Julinia, the guard is on the march.
    And with thy father's fiat now in force,
    If thou art seen thou wilt be herded here to home.

JULINIA
    Then I shall don regalia of a grunt 155
    Lest I be shunted from the vital task.
    And with my sex secreted neath this mask,
    Into the breach I go, to sally forth—but as a joe.

HIPPOPOTIMA
    Godspeed, Julinia.
    I will pray and eat for your safe return. 160

JULINIA
    Remember, Hippy,
    No puny dictums of a man
    Would stay a cat once fixed upon her way.
    And those who rule by virtue
    Of their lofty dangly bits 165
    Will e'er be underminéd
    By the she who wears the tits.

                                                    [*Exeunt.*]

3.2 As Hameo and Schmuck approach Castle Bolingbras, Schmuck suggests that Hameo disguise himself, since the guard is out searching the forest for him, and magically provides Hameo with the garb of a milkmaid. Julinia, disguised as a soldier, discovers Hameo and the two are oddly attracted to one another despite believing the other to be of the opposite sex. They then reveal their true identities and head off to the castle to save Lymetrius.

1-3. **We've foot-slogged over ruddy yards...din:** referring to Rudyard Kipling's 1890 poem, *Gunga Din*.

3. **breadless basket:** empty stomach

21. **sung and jung a jango:** something that Muskrat Susie and Muskrat Sam like to do in the 1976 Captain & Tennille hit *Muskrat Love*.

22. **went upon his macrodonic way:** macrodontia; big teeth

3.2 *Enter Hameo and Schmuck.*

HAMEO
  We've foot-slogged over ruddy yards for miles
  Without a bite or swig of the canteen
  To quell the o, so breadless basket's din.
  And seemingly no farther from our start
  Than we've become the nearer to our end. 5

SCHMUCK
  Well then so very wrong thou art, my friend.
  For just beyond the cusp of wood and brush
  Lies thy beleaguered bud, Lymetrius,
  Imprisoned by the brutal Bolingbras
  Whose savage realm we've only just transpierced. 10

HAMEO
  How come thee by thy knowledge?

SCHMUCK
  A muskrat, as I'm fluent in his tongue,
  Did eek to me his cautionary tale.
  A royal unit, thrusting through the rushes,
  Uncivilly crushed his home of sticks and mud 15
  As they did comb the conifers to find
  Some sign of the confederate unto some captive sap.
  Methinks the chap they ferret for be thee.

HAMEO
  But does Lymetrius yet live?

SCHMUCK
  The fraternizing rat was loath to say, 20
  He merely sung and jung a jango
  Then went upon his macrodonic way.

HAMEO
  Then quick, we must seek shelter lest we be discoveréd.

SCHMUCK
  The guard of Bolingbras is quite adept.
  No matter where you're squirreléd 25
  They soon 'twould have your nuts.

38-46. Abracadabra...Alakazam...Sim Sala Bim... Hocus Pocus: These are incantations used as magic words. Some other famous incantations, not used but considered for this text were: *Shazam*, *Presto Chango*, *Bibbidi-Bobbidi-Boo*, *Supercalifragilisticexpialidocious*, *Wonder Twin powers activate,* and *Oo ee oo ah ah ting tang walla walla bing bang.*

And so, no buts, you must adhere to me
And thus conceal thyself for all to see.

HAMEO
Riddle me not thou impish potpourri.

SCHMUCK
I'll be more plain, as time is tight for thee.
My sage advice that I do bid thee heed,
Is that thou'd best be hid beneath another hide.

HAMEO
And where should such a camouflage be forthwith found?

SCHMUCK
My lord, lest thou forget,
Thou travelst with a pygmy paranormalist.
Now, swift from sight behind the shrubbery
As thine old semblance I transmogrify.
Now bear with me, I'm a bit rusty. Abracadabra!

HAMEO
No.

SCHMUCK
Alakazam.

HAMEO
No!!

SCHMUCK
Sim Sala Bim.

HAMEO
Nothin'.

SCHMUCK
Bim...Sala Sim?

HAMEO
Oh for God's sake.

SCHMUCK
Hold on, hold on, I'm getting it. Hocus Pocus.

51. **Stephanopoulos:** referring to Clinton senior advisor and political commentator George Stephanopoulos, whose last name is such a mouthful it might as well have magical powers.

52. **Klaatu Barada Nikto**: spoken as a order to stand down to Gort, the planet annihilating robot of the 1951 film *The Day The Earth Stood Still*.

54-55. **Bricka-Bracka Firecracker. Sis Boom Bah!:** If you are not familiar with the genius of Warner Bros. animator Chuck Jones then go sing some Looney Tunes and Merrie Melodies as soon as possible.

HAMEO
  Nope.

SCHMUCK
  Alakazam.

HAMEO
  Ya did that one already!!! Jesus!

SCHMUCK
  OK. I'm breaking out the hard stuff.
  Uh...Stephanopoulos. Shish Kabob.
  Klaatu Barada Nikto.

HAMEO
  I'm going to hurt you.

SCHMUCK
  Bricka-bracka Firecracker, Sis-Boom-Bah.
  Bugs Bunny, Bugs Bunny, Rah, Rah, Rah!

HAMEO
  Should I shoot him now or wait till I get home?
  Shoot him now. Shoot him now.

SCHMUCK
  Ah ha!

  [*Twitches nose accompanied by "Bewitched" sound effect.*]

HAMEO
  Art thou a witch?

SCHMUCK
  What.

HAMEO
  Art thou a witch!?!

SCHMUCK
  No.

  [*Hameo reaches out and smacks Schmuck in the head.*]

66. **your pornstar name:** No one is really quite sure how the concept of creating a pornstar name by adding a pet name to a street name began or, for that matter, why all performers in the porn industry are considered "stars" in the first place. My pornstar name would be *Bobo Dalewood*—which actually sounds kinda hot!

77. **But soft, what knight...breaks?:** refers to the line "But soft, What light through yonder window breaks" from Shakespeare's *Romeo and Juliet*.

SCHMUCK
I got it. I got it. (*to audience member.*)
You got a pet? What's its name?
OK, now what street did you grow up on?
Great. That's your pornstar name.
OK, we're goin' with the pornstar name.
You said (*fill in the blank.*), our survey said...

[*Hameo emerges from shrubbery in a milkmaid dress.*]

HAMEO
You have got to be kidding me.

SCHMUCK
But none could fabricate a finer bluff.
Not only masked is thine identity,
But should the guard engage this lovely lass,
Thy counterfeit, for fear she'd be imperiléd,
Would be escorted straight betwixt
The gates of Bolingbras.

HAMEO
O, so be it. There is design to thy dementia.
But soft, what knight through yonder bushes breaks?
It is the beastly guard of Bolingbras
Too soon upon our heels.
Then let us put our stratagem on wheels.
Fly hence!

SCHMUCK
I'm coming with you.

HAMEO
No, I go with the guard and you go puck yourself.

[*Exit Schmuck.*]

Enter Julinia, as guard.

HAMEO
Good sir!

JULINIA
Ahhhhhhh!!!!!

101-2. **Thy beauty...the rigor of his mortis:** The state of rigor mortis is characterized by a chemical reaction in muscle tissue causing a stiffening of the limbs. Whether this process extends to all appendages is unknown.

HAMEO
  A thousand pardons that I thee alarm.

JULINIA
  No, no, fair lady. 'Tis but a signal to the regiment.
  Ahhhhh! He is not hither!!
  Ahhhhh! I'll search him elseways!!

GUARD (O.S.)
  Shut up! You'll scare him off!!

JULINIA
  Sorry!! (*to Hameo*) But wherefore dost thou roam
  These wild woods without the benefit of chaperonage?
  Dear maid, art thou mad? A villain's on the loose.

HAMEO
  Alas, I'm but a senseless wench
  Without the wits that God bestowed a chicken.
  And yet when thinking runs afoul of affairs,
  My paltry poultry brain doth e'er surmise
  Salvation's but spit distance of my plight.
  It takes the form and guise of rugged dudes
  Ensnaréd by my ample pulchritude.

JULINIA
  'Tis true. Thy beauty, even to a man deceased,
  Wouldst yet increase the rigor of his mortis.
  But I am fixed upon a royal charge,
  As there is yet a lunatic at large,
  And cannot deviate beyond my noble course.

HAMEO
  Well, I never!...well, sometimes...OK, a lot!
  But it means not that thou canst treat me as a whore.
  What kind of man art thou?

JULINIA
  ('Tis a good question.)

HAMEO
  A curvy wench as I thou wouldst leave flat?
  Thy oath as man 'tis "shield the fairer sex,"
  Which all doth know o'ercedes that to a king.

116-34. **balls?...I most certainly have balls:** Is there a writer who could not for page after page wax poetic about a truly majestic set of love-nuggets? From Keats' *Ode on a Grecian Vas Deferens* to Frost's *The Scrot Not Taken* to Thomas's haunting *Do Not Go Genital Into That Good Night*, great artists the world over have paid homage to huevos for as long a man has put quill to papyrus.

Wouldst thou abjure for fear of sovereignty?
Oh my, what gall!
Forgive, but I must ask thee, hast thou balls? 115

JULINIA
Balls? Why yes, I have balls.
Those potent orbs of masculinity
That o so gently glide betwixt my stride.
Two... (*aside.*) It is two right?
(*To Hameo*) Yes, two spheric grand progenitors of man. 120
And what a piece of work are they.
How infinite in faculty. In action, watch out.
In apprehension, like a shriveled bag of prunes.
But they are my balls.
There are many like them but these are mine. 125
Without me, my balls are useless.
Without my balls, I am useless.
We are defenders of my country
And master of our enemy.
And yes, should I so choose, 130
I can sling 'em over my shoulder
Like a continental soldier.
So test thee not my testes.
For I most certainly have balls.

HAMEO
Me thinks thou dost affirm to much. 135

JULINIA
Oh dost thou?

HAMEO
Yeah, I dost.

JULINIA
Be careful where thou'st tread.

HAMEO
Mean thee upon thy phantom 'nads?

JULINIA
Do watch thy tongue, for quite man am I. 140

150. **siren's song:** In Greek mythology, the Sirens were dangerous creatures, who lured nearby sailors with their enchanting music and singing voices to shipwreck on the rocky coast of their island. They were like the Taylor Swifts of their day—but with less drama.

154. **my immaculate canoe:** When a woman lands her canoe upon the shores of Lesbos, the little man within it will undoubtedly receive a warm reception.

159. **I'm not akin unto this band of village people:** a '70s group known for their catchy tunes and homoerotic lyrics, *Village People* created such hits singles as "In the Navy" and "Y.M.C.A."

Photo # NH 56679   U.S. Frigate Boston in the Mediterranean, circa 1802. Engraving by Baugean

HAMEO
  Then prove it thus.
                              [*Julinia grabs Hameo.
                              They kiss, then separate.*]

JULINIA (*aside.*)
  Oh God!

HAMEO (*aside.*)
  Oh hell!

JULINIA (*aside.*)
  What damnifying turpitude is this?

HAMEO (*aside.*)
  More heinous than relations with your sis.   145

JULINIA (*aside.*)
  Lord knows, I should be cast in the abyss...

HAMEO/JULINIA (*aside.*)
  And yet...

JULINIA (*aside.*)
  I'd be forsworn denying her allure.

HAMEO (*aside.*)
  This lad did stir a cogent primal urge.

JULINIA (*aside.*)
  Ne'er didst methink I'd heed a siren's song,   150
  Whose lyrics ne'er I've been susceptive to.
  Methought I'd berth upon the Isle of Man.
  Not let the shore of Lesbos come
  To wreak the wreck of my immaculate canoe.

HAMEO (*aside.*)
  'Tis queer for one as masculine as me   155
  To be enticed by like homology.
  Such deviance doth not befit my rank.
  'Tis more the province of the common folk.
  I'm not akin unto this band of village people.

JULINIA
  My lady, do forgive of my offense.   160

167. **I fear my dear canoe doth take on water:** When one's lovely canoe is jostled or this vessel takes on ballast, a gentle mist may dampen her port side.

174. **nosh:** to snack or eat between meals. *"Hey Fat Elvis impersonator, you eat so much you must be from Noshville, Tennessee."*

175. **place the kibosh on:** to put an end to; squelch. *"If you don't stop doing that I will kibosh you on the head with my guitar like El Kabong!"*

HAMEO
This colorful behavior's a disgrace beyond the pale.

JULINIA
Agreed, it was egregious.

HAMEO
Then of it let us speak no more.

JULINIA
As you desire.

HAMEO
Now where were we. 165

[They kiss once more.]

HAMEO (*aside.*)
Should this be wrong, ne'er wouldst I dare be right.

[They kiss.]

JULINIA (*aside.*)
I fear my dear canoe doth take on water.

[They kiss.]

HAMEO
My love, I shant deny my sentiment.

JULINIA
Thy lips are bliss and irresistible.
And since my love for thee is love unbounded, 170
I'm thus compelled to now reveal a truth
That may, when so declared, leave thee confounded.

HAMEO
No matter what deceptive dish thou serve,
If mon amour be but the chef, I'll nosh.
For nought could place the kibosh on our love. 175

JULINIA
I prithee, avert thine eyes for sake of modesty.
And know thee whenst I speak of my desire
To draw thee near and cleave unto my bosom,
I speak to thee not in the figurative.
For all I have to give I give to thee. 180
But give it not as him but as a she.

[Julinia removes uniform to reveal herself.]

184. **hung with privates:** If you hung with privates, the Rear Admiral may want a word with you on the poop deck.

187. **Despite a lack of tackle or an old kit-bag?:** You can pack all your troubles in your old kit-bag, and smile. But if you pack all of your old kit-bag in somebody's smile, you may be in trouble.

188. **The standard of my love has yet to flag:** *standard* —1. an established model or example; 2. war flag.

191. **Holland's Haarlem hero...brink, Her:** refers to *Hans Brinker, or the Silver Skates*, and the story within about the little Dutch boy who put his finger in the dyke.

196. **dexter also ambi?:** referring to the word *ambidextrous*—able to use the right or left hand equally well or, in this case, go one way or the other.

210. **iambic fucking pentameter:** metrical line in English poetry and verse drama in which five sets of stressed and unstressed syllables or iambs are employed. The sets are also called "feet" because the mental gymnastics required to create one of these iambic pentametric lines feels like someone kicking you in the balls five times.

HAMEO
  Methought thy lip too soft
  And skin too fair by far
  For one who hung with privates.

JULINIA
  But generally speaking, 185
  Wouldst thou still soldier on with a romance
  Despite a lack of tackle or an old kit-bag?

HAMEO
  The standard of my love has yet to flag.
  Forsooth, thy present form has more appeal
  Than that which thou hast chosen to conceal. 190

JULINIA
  Like Holland's Haarlem hero famed to all,
  Just as our damned romance was on the brink,
  Her saintly hand didst deign to save our love
  And sweetly thrust a digit in the dyke.
  Forgive if this inquiry's namby-pamby, 195
  But is my lovely's dexter also ambi?

HAMEO
  The portal to my heart swings but one way;
  It swings to thee. For I too have a secret to reveal.
  And though 'tis odd for two deceits
  To so well harmonize, 200
  Like some pitiful contrivance
  Of a most unworthy scribe...

Enter Playwright.

PLAYWRIGHT
  Ho! Ho! Time out here. Unworthy scribe?
  Unworthy scribe? Where do you get off?
  You think this shit is easy? You try it. 205
  There's no carousin' for me. I'm not going to cast parties.
  I'm not fuckin' drunk actresses.
  I'm the guy sittin' at a desk, day and night,
  Scratching away, trying to make you look good.
  And in iambic fucking pentameter no less. Contrived? 210

215. **Boy writes himself into his own play:** Why should I just limit myself to commenting on this work here in these explanatory notes when I can actually insert myself into the show and comment on it there too? Pretty ingenious if you ask me.

217. **play with their thumbs:** referring to Gene Siskel and Roger Ebert of the television series *At the Movies*, in which they would rate movies with a "thumbs up" or "thumbs down."

232. **mine own concoction well in hand:** In this event, one will usually have a stroke of good luck which will lead to a happy ending.

Yeah, it's contrived. Everything's contrived.
As soon as it comes outta my head and hits the page
It's contrived. Hell, there's only ever been five original
Stories written—ever! Boy meets girl. Boy loses girl.
Boy writes himself into his own play. It's all been done.
So why don't you just stick to the acting and we'll let
The critics play with their thumbs. OK?

HAMEO
Yeah, but...you wrote "unworthy scribe."

PLAYWRIGHT
Oh. Oh, I see. So now it's my fault, huh?
Boy, you've got some set of brass ones don't ya?
You better watch yourself, 'cause I can pull this play
Just like that—it's in my contract. Now let's get on with it.
We got a house full of folks here that didn't pay
Good money to get dicked around by the likes of you.
Sheesh, actors.

[Exit Playwright.]

HAMEO
Right. Now where were we? Oh yeah, I got it...
Two deceit's to so well harmonize, like some...
Well...you know.
'Twould seem upon us fate doth wryly smile,
For all the while as thou didst veil thy sex
And weave this fabrication of a gent,
I had mine own concoction well in hand
And thus beneath this fabric lies a man.

[Hameo disrobes to reveal yet another dress.]

Puck! I'm gonna get ya, ya little son of a bitch!!

*[Hameo rips off the second dress.
They kiss once more.]*

JULINIA
But wherefore didst thou so conceal thyself?

HAMEO
'Twas Schmuck, an impish kin to Tinkerbell,
Whose magic tailoréd this frickin' frock,
That I might sail past soldiers on my way

241. **best bro:** a figurative "brother" or best friend—like BFF, main man, bestie, chum, buddy, broseph, wingman, dogg, homey or home slice.

266. **Vera Wang:** American fashion designer and former editor of *Vogue* magazine.

To save my friend, my poor Lymetrius,
Who's trussed up in the hold of Bolingbras.
Should I not have the back of my best bro
Then call me not the name Prince Hameo.

JULINIA
Then thou art just the man for whom I seek,
Yea all my life, but this day otherwise.
I am Princess Julinia you see,
Daughter to the king thou so oppose.
Though know thee with the throne I'm not allied.
In sooth, I tried to help thy hapless friend.
Alas, my act of aiding and abetting
May soon conclude, I fear, in his beheading.
And since my best intentions turned to plight,
I sought thee, so disguised, to make things right.

HAMEO
Then we must readorn ourselves posthaste.
To waste away the day with idle chat
'Twould mean my dear friend's life's not worth a chit.

JULINIA
No Hameo, there is no time for that.
Besides, that gags a bit played out already
Don't ya think?

HAMEO
Yeah, I guess. Been there, done that.

JULINIA
Now swift, we must unto the castle steal.
We'll tread a path known only to my heel
And slip right past the guard upon this route
And then save dear Lymetrius to boot.
Say, do you think that little magic dude
Could crank-out that dress in my size?
Cause it's really got this whole kinda Vera Wang
Thing happening there and I think it would really...
Oh, I'm sorry. Your friend's gonna die and...
Well look, we'll talk later.

[Exeunt.]

3.3 Hameo and Julinia are captured and thrown into the dungeon along with Lymetrius by the jailkeepers, Rosenstern and Guildencrantz. Lymetrius apologizes for losing Hameo's gold and introduces him to his beloved nostril hair. Schmuck appears at the dungeon window but, despite Hameo's command, is unable to magically free them from captivity. He suggests they join forces with the other prisoners, the players, a rap group that will be performing for the king later that evening. Our three heroes slip out with the players when they are called to the stage by disguising themselves as part of the group—with the knowledge and bemusement of Rosenstern and Guildencrantz.

3-4. **companionship...paramour to misery:** referring to the adage "misery loves company."

9-10. **pinned us to thy tail...equally assigned us:** an allusion to the game, *Pin the Tail on the Donkey*. The Latin binomial nomenclature for donkey is *Equus Asinus*.

11-17. **The one less traveled by...in fire:** This section is a play on two poems by Robert Frost. This first, *The Road Not Taken*, contains the passage, "I kept the first for another day" and "I shall be telling this with a sigh somewhere ages and ages hence: Two roads diverged in a wood, and I—I took the one less traveled by, and that made all the difference." The second, *Fire and Ice*, contains the line, "Some say the world will end in fire, some say in ice."

3.3 *Enter Rosenstern. Lymetrius sits, imprisoned.*
The Players sleep under cover.

ROSENSTERN
Good eventide, my little detainee.
I have for thee a wonder to behold.

Enter Guildencrantz, Hameo and Julinia.

A few old chums for some companionship—
The oft reported paramour to misery.

JULINIA
The king shall have your heads for this affront.

ROSENSTERN
I more suspect a pat upon the back.

GUILDENCRANTZ
The only sword betwixt our shoulder blades
'Twould be the one to knight us with a tap,
For 'twas thy dad who pinned us to thy tail
And equally assigned us to the task
As he too is quite savvy of thy trail within the wood—
The one less travel by.

ROSENSTERN
And that made all the difference, should thou ask.

GUILDENCRANTZ
So keep thy threatenings for another day,
'Cause I can tell ye now without a sigh,
You'll be here till the world has turned to frost.

ROSENSTERN
Of course, some say it'll end in fire—
But that's neither here nor there.

HAMEO
You know, thou dost remindeth me...

GUILDENCRANTZ
Oh no, not he.

HAMEO
And thou art but the image and the spit...

24-25. Rosenzweig...charming sisters: referring to the play by Wendy Wasserstein, *The Sisters Rosensweig*.

26-27. Gildersleeve...he's quite a fibber: referring to *The Great Gildersleeve*, a 1940s radio situation comedy featuring the character Throckmorton P. Gildersleeve. (The show was a spin-off program from the radio comedy, *Fibber McGee and Molly*.)

37-39. left me but a shell...a hull, a husk...Oh shucks: *Shucks* is an expression of mild disappointment or embarrassment but also the removal of shells, hulls and husks. A *shuck*, as a noun, is also a shell or husk.

40. outtrumps the gold...an apprentice...you're fired: referring, of course, to Donald Trump and his penchant for gold décor, his show *The Apprentice,* and his catch phrase, "You're fired." (I was actually concerned that in years to come people might not get this reference as Donald Trump was relegated to the dustbin of history—then he became President of the United States; God help us all.)

ROSENSTERN
What him? No, not a bit.

GUILDENCRANTZ
Do let us introduce ourselves.
He's known throughout the land as Rosenzweig.

ROSENSTERN
As are my charming sisters.   25
And this here's my compadre Gildersleeve.
He's quite a fibber; cross my liver.

GUILDENCRANTZ
We'll be your captors this evening.

ROSENSTERN
If there's anything, anything at all we can do
To make your stay less comfortable, do let us know.   30

[*Exeunt Rosenstern and Guildencrantz.*]

HAMEO
How now, Lymetrius? I pray that thou art free of injury.

LYMETRIUS
In praise of God, I am as yet unharmed,
Still crippled all the same by sense of shame.
To wager on the placement of a pea,
To stake the ducats thou entrusted me,   35
Then cowardly to flee from thy recourse.
This game of shells has left me but a shell.
No man here dwells. I'm but a hull, a husk.

HAMEO
Oh shucks, Lymetrius.
Our well-worn friendship far outtrumps the gold.   40
Thou, but an apprentice wert to worldly ways.
But now, you're fired in its crucible,
And hence, distinguish dreams from cold reality.
So do arise and come embrace me well.
For I thee tell there is no wrong of thine   45
That labors hard for Hercules,

56. **Oh, been reading page 27 have we?:** I'm sure by now you've looked back in the script and have discovered that the actions describes actually took place between page 93 and 103 of this book. In the originally stage script, which didn't have these explanatory notes and was more tightly spaced, the actions took place between page 28 and 31—closer, but not the page 27 mentioned earlier by Hameo and here by Lymetrius. Look, I just liked the sound of "page 27." Let's not get all bent out of shape about it, OK?

61-62. **Screw Stanislavski...Uta, blow me:** Konstantin Stanislavski, Sanford Meisner, and Uta Hagen were all renowned acting teachers and proponents of "method acting."

Lifelong indentured servitude,
And garnishment of wage cannot assuage.

LYMETRIUS
Thy magnanimity is truly grand.
(Exceeded solely by how fucked I am.)
But on to other matters.
Let me now recount my anecdotes
Since we've diverged.

HAMEO
My thanks, but thou need not elucidate.
I have been dished the dirt by other means.

LYMETRIUS
Oh, been reading page 27 have we?

HAMEO
Shhhh!!

Enter Playwright.

PLAYWRIGHT
No-nuh-nuh-no. It's a little too late for shush.
I got ears like a...I don't know...something that hears good.
So, you like jumping around in the script, huh?
Can't just be in the moment. Screw Stanislavski,
Fuck Meisner, Uta?—blow me. I gotta know everything.
I gotta play God. That's it. From now on,
Everybody gets sides.

JULINIA (*aside.*)
For those not versed in theatrical terminology,
Traditionally, sides were abbreviated scripts with only
An individual actors lines and just the preceding cues.

PLAYWRIGHT
Hey! These are theatre people. They know what sides are.
I've had it. I got a case of Stoli backstage.
I think I'm gonna pour me a pool of it and go take a swim.
Say, that's pretty good. I think I'm gonna
Have to use that sometime.

[*Exit Playwright.*]

75-81. entangled with...sheer delight...old and grey: "Let it fly in the breeze and get caught in the trees, make a home for the flees in my hair."—Ragni/Rado

88. Nyeh, could be: It is impossible to have too many Bugs Bunny references.

90. homunculitic halfwit: A *homunculus* is a diminutive form of man or scale model of a human.

LYMETRIUS
   Since thou already hast divined my tale,
   Allow me to unveil my bride to be.

                 [*Lymetrius reveals the nostril hair.*]

HAMEO
   So here's the hair thy heart's entangled with. 75
   And what a lovely little lock is she.

LYMETRIUS
   Why yes, I must agree; a sheer delight.
   And yet our love's for nought
   If we're to perish in this hold.
   So gather up thy wits, for from this brig we must away, 80
   Allowing that together we may yet turn old and grey.

JULINIA
   Alas, this castle for an eon stood her ground.
   And ne'er within this age hath yet
   A so resolved incarcerant to cheat these mossy walls,
   Except to tunnel into madness or skedaddle into death. 85

        Enter Schmuck outside barred window.

SCHMUCK
   Boy, ain't she a barrel of monkeys.

JULINIA
   Why thou must be the puck, ally to Hameo.

SCHMUCK (*chewing carrot à la Bugs Bunny.*)
   Nyeh, could be.

HAMEO
   We've scarce the time for antics,
   Thou homunculitic halfwit. Employ thy sorcery 90
   Upon the bolt or cookie dough the door to dust
   Or chocolate jimmie up the latch
   Or smite it with a pixie stick.
   I care not what confection thou must wield
   But wield it now and do it quick. 95

SCHMUCK
   Alas, as I'm a creature of the wood,
   My enigmatic power's compromised

101. **I don't do windows:** Many maids will tell you they don't do windows but apparently certain pucks are equally disinclined to perform such menial tasks.

118. **cuckoo for Cocoa Puffs:** the tagline of Sonny the Cuckoo Bird, mascot for the General Mills chocolatey breakfast cereal *Cocoa Puffs*. Colloquially, if you refer to someone as "cuckoo for Cocoa Puff" you would be suggesting that they are fucking insane.

Should I engage my skills against its source,
The very wood from which it is derived.

HAMEO
And what of this metallic barricade? 100

SCHMUCK
I don't do windows. But I have news for thee.
The word of thy confinement's echoed home,
And denizens have raised a cry and hue
That Milhous should debut his regal might,
Demanding a safe passage for the prince 105
And too his noble entourage.
He'll soon arrive for soft diplomacy,
And Bolingbras pays homage to thy king
And honors him this night with festival.
But he'll be not dissuade by pleasantries. 110
Thy uncle will pursue a call to arms
If but a single hair should come to harm.

LYMETRIUS (*to Nostril Hair*)
Do this thou hear, my love?
Ah, would that thou had ears for fetching words.
No single hair shall come to harm, so says the king. 115
Though thou with me be single hair no more.

SCHMUCK
Hey Hammy, eh, nothin' for nothin',
But I think your boy's a little cuckoo for Cocoa Puffs
Over here, if ya know what I mean.

HAMEO
Tell me about it. But now to this, 120
For all my senses say it is amiss;
Old Milhous toward such ends for my deliverance?
I fear I'd ponder at the prospect,
Yea, long past the point when Bolingbras
Doth separate my ponderer from my personage. 125

SCHMUCK
My lord, if I might be allowed a thought.
Perhaps salvation lies though joint endeavor

133. **heef:** As a further example, hoof is to heef in the same way as roof is to reef.

140. **a wandering band of theater folk:** This strolling troupe was once on a seven city tour of Italy but, apparently, didn't really care for their time in Parma—referring to it repeatedly as a menace.

147-48. **achieve our liberty...poor huddled mass:** The quote at the base of the Statue of Liberty reads "Give me your tired, your poor, your huddled masses yearning to breathe free"—just in case you wanted to know. Not sure if this plaque is still there at the time of your reading. I believe a certain political party was in the process of trying to have it removed.

With those others over yonder
Who now do slumber under cover.
For now must I depart, as men of war   130
Will soon be chomping at my heef.

HAMEO
Thy what?

SCHMUCK
My heef. You know, the plural of hoof.
Foot, feet; hoof, heef—get it?

HAMEO
You're an idiot. Ya know that, don't you?   135

SCHMUCK
I do beseech the gods this storm ye weather.
But if 'twere not to be, it was a pleasure.

HAMEO
Why you little...

    [*Exit Schmuck.*]

What retched souls are these that share the ground?

LYMETRIUS
They are a wandering band of theatre folk.   140
They last performed for Bolingbras a fortnight past.

HAMEO
It wouldst appear their notices were poor.

JULINIA
They are to yet again perform this night.
And should the king find displeasure 'pon the stage,
For them it will assuredly be curtains.   145

HAMEO
As our capricious puck put forth,
We may achieve our liberty with aid from this
Poor, huddled mass. Arise and introduce thyself.

TOP DOG
Yo yo yo, my royal bro. We is the players.

The Players: The name of each of the players relates to the characters of workmen who perform "Pyramus and Thisbe," which is a play within the play *A Midsummer Night's Dream*: Top Dog/Bottom; Q-Tip/Quince; Snotrag/Snout; Hashpipe/Flute; Snuggy Bear/Snug; Starvin' Marvin/Starveling.

Q-Tip: The character of Q-Tip (a personal favorite) is a homage to Damon Waynes' *In Living Color* creation, Oswald Bates, a prison inmate who speaks in excessively flowery malaprops in an attempt to project sophistication.

150. **perspicacity:** keenness of mental perception

151. **cognifify:** understand

162. **At your cervix:** If one provides you with good cervix, it would be appropriate to leave them a nice tip.

167. **extremulated unfortutude:** great sorrow

168. **unquenchinable:** unassuageable

Q-TIP
 As thou, with thine abundant perspicacity,
 Canst clearly cognifify.

HASHPIPE
 What he say, yo.

SNUGGY BEAR
 Where the bitches at?

HAMEO
 Their language, as its origins, is colorful indeed.

TOP DOG
 Now here's a little roll call fo y'all.
 Check it. Top Dog.

Q-TIP
 Q-Tip.

HASHPIPE
 Hashpipe.

SNUGGY BEAR
 Snuggy Bear.

SNOTRAG
 Snotrag.

STARVIN' MARVIN
 And Starvin' Marvin.

SNUGGY BEAR (*to Julinia.*)
 At your cervix.

 [*He puts his head under her skirt.*]

HAMEO
 Unmouth her highness thou heinous
 And most crass rapscallion.

TOP DOG
 My lady, do accept of me 3865 and a half pardons
 On behalf of my fellow cast member.

Q-TIP
 It is with the most extremulated unfortutude
 That I must convey to thee the unquenchinable

169. **libidinosity:** the act of being horny; **compeer:** comrade and peer

170. **exacerfied:** exacerbated; **proxsiquity:** proximity

171. **pulchritute:** an attractive woman; **vernaculus:** vernacular

172. **antithetical:** opposite; **sexification:** gender

174. **recompense**: compensation for an injury, wrong or injustice.

179. **tyros:** a beginner in learning anything; novice

183. **Grand Poobah:** a term derived from the name of the haughty character Pooh-Bah in Gilbert and Sullivan's *The Mikado*, who held many lofty titles. Also the name of a high-ranking elected position in a secret society, the Loyal Order of Water Buffaloes, in the television show *The Flintstones*.

Libidinosity of our beloved compeer, which is
Exacerfied whenst he's in direct proxsinquity 170
With a pulchritute, or in Snuggy Bear's vernaculus,
"Hot bitch," of the antithetical sexification.

HAMEO
Is there a thesaurus in the house?

JULINIA
Apologies are best express in deeds of recompense,
Not feather-weighted words, those hollow seeds 175
That light on fallow ground and come to nought.
I charge thee now, for thine amends,
Do aid in our abscondance.

STARVIN' MARVIN
Well, thou knowst we ain't no tyros
Whenst it comes to being charged. 180

SNOTRAG
Charged, yea—but ne'er convicted.

TOP DOG (*rapping.*)
May I say to thee
As Grand Poobah of this crew,
That what of which thou need
Be that of which we do. 185
And all my homies and me
Art prepared to take a fall,
As we wouldst e'er to be
At thy dispose y'all.

STARVIN' MARVIN
Word to thy matriarch. 190

HASHPIPE
Consider this a toke of our esteem, yo.

HAMEO
Then gather for my genius stroke
Which thusly will proceed.

[*Hameo, Julinia, Lymetrius and the Players*
huddle and murmur in discussion.]

200. **popo at the do', mofo:** police at the door, motherfucker

205. **my three chums:** an allusion to the '60s television show *My Three Sons*.

207. **interjeculate:** interject

208. **expetageous:** expedient and advantageous

209. **unabridgedly:** thoroughly; **oclify:** search

210. **posthastedly:** quickly; **unignorated:** enlightened

211. **troika:** a grouping of three; **incarcemates:** incarcerated inmates

212. **inquisified:** asked

213. **in a dormantic state:** sleeping

214. **terra firma:** ground

SNUGGY BEAR
  Forsooth, knowst well that I do grip the scheme.
  Though to my bean, there's but a quite minute   195
  Yet salient factor till this point left unspoke.

HAMEO
  And that wouldst be?

SNUGGY BEAR
  Where art there be the nearest and most
  Amply capacious repository of bitches?

TOP DOG
  Yo, yo, yo! We's got the popo at do', mofo.   200

  Enter Rosenstern and Guildencrantz.

ROSENSTERN
  Come players, you've been summoned to the stage
  For what I figs your final gig, I'll wage.

GUILDENCRANTZ
  Now hold your pie, Rosensweig.

ROSENSTERN
  Well, what's thy peeve, Gildersleeve?

GUILDENCRANTZ
  I say to thee, what then hast become of my three chums?   205
  The princess and her escort, plus the other one?

Q-TIP
  If I might introjeculate at this juncture,
  It wouldst be most expetageous for ye
  To unabridgedly oclify thy vicinity.
  Then thou wouldst be posthastedly unignorated   210
  To the fact that the troika of incarcemates,
  Of which thou hast inquisified,
  Art in a dormantic state o'er yonder
  'Pon the terra firma.

SNOTRAG
  Down the ground, yo.   215

216. **In futhertude:** furthermore; **ginormous:** huge; **corporeal:** physical

217. **psych-somaticological:** relating to the mind-body connect; **stressifications:** strain

218. **malfoodlums:** ruffians or criminals; **siestafied:** sleeping

219. **indefisable perpetude:** indeterminable time

234-35. **Thou art good...yea, thou dost:** a play on a line from Robert DeNiro's character, Paul Vitti, in the film *Analyze This*

236. **homage:** here pronounced *oh-MAZH*

239. **That's right. That's right. We bad:** from the film *Stir Crazy* (1980)—a scene in which Gene Wilder and Richard Pryor are trying to act tough in prison

Q-TIP
  In furthertude, by merit of ginormous corporeal
  And psycho-somaticological stressifications,
  These here malfoodlums may well be siestafied
  For an indefisable perpetude.

SNOTRAG
  Catchin' Zs, yo.

TOP DOG (*rapping.*)
  So let's not be keepin' the royals
  Or makin 'em stew in the vat.
  Y'all investigating a problem
  That ain't harmin' a nat.
  We got to go, be out the do',
  Rev up the show, bro.
  'Hearse, clean up the verse,
  Don't make me curse, yo.
  Why don't ya'll just chill
  And let my sleepin' dogs lie
  And we'll be jumpin' up on the stage
  To give us brothers a try. Shit.

HASHPIPE (*aside.*)
  Come on, give it to the man. Give it till it hurt.

ROSENSTERN (*to Top Dog, à la DeNiro.*)
  Thou. Thou art good. No, thou art good, thou.
  Thou hast a gift. Yea thou dost. Yea thou dost.

GUILDENCRANTZ
  Do let us shuttle this homage upon its way
  Or 'mongst the heads plucked by the throne
  We two may find our very own.

                              [*Exeunt the Players.*]

              [*Hameo, Lymetrius and Julinia are revealed
                     in Rastafarian caps with dreadlocks.*]

JULINIA
  That's right. That's right. We bad.

                         [*Exeunt Hameo, Lymetrius and Julinia.*]

242. **rinky-dinks:** a group of little importance or value
243. **Lamb-eyed:** pull the wool over one's eyes

3.4 Milhous and Bolingbras, after dispatching a servant and the Duke of Bilgewater, engage in a pact, whereby each will kill the other's nephew and daughter, respectively, initiating a justifiable war between their peoples so they might tax and rob them of their wealth. They embrace and prepare for an evening of theater and festival.

GUILDENCRANTZ (*aside.*)
  That, I surmise, is the worst disguise 240
  That I have yet beheld.

ROSENSTERN (*aside.*)
  Lest ye should think these rinky-dinks
  Lamb-eyed us from this cell.

GUILDENCRANTZ (*aside.*)
  Then why, ye may inquire,
  Didst we let them in the game? 245

ROSENSTERN (*aside.*)
  We don't make much and so as such
  This keeps us entertained.

[*Exeunt.*]

3.4 *Enter King Milhous, Bilgewater,*
Servants and Bolingbras.

[*Flourish: Hail to the Chief*]

SERVANT
  Greetings to thee, King Milhous.
  You do afford great honor unto the court of
  Bolingbras with your serendipitous arrival.
  Do grant us pardon your approach was not
  Rose-petaled and the moatbridge was 5
  Left uncleared of dung this day.
  Had we known you'd come it wouldst be done.

KING MILHOUS
  Do think thee nought of it.

[*Knees the Servant in the loins,*
wipes right foot on him.]

  And the other one.

[*Gestures to roll over,*
then wipes left foot.]

SERVANT
  Thank you, your majesty. I'm graced by this debasement. 10

KING MILHOUS
  Ah, Bolingbras.
  I trust that I have not o'erstepped decorum
  In the treatment of thy footrag as a footman.

15. **Me groveling...es su:** Why should someone only be deemed gracious by offering their *casa*?

18-19. **my fiend and confidant:** As the saying goes, "a fiend in need is a fiend indeed."

31. **proles:** a shortening of the word *proletariat* or working class.

BOLINGBRAS
  Why Milhous, thou dost know me well enough.
  Me groveling, ass-wiping, worthless,
  Subhuman wretch of a peon es su...
  Whatever I just said, repeated.

KING MILHOUS
  I believe thou art acquainted with my fiend
  And confidant, the Duke of Bilgewater.

BILGEWATER
  Your majesty.

BOLINGBRAS
  Why yes, dear Bilgewater. The honor is all yours.
  Well then Milhous, let us to the purpose of thy jaunt.
  Thy nephew and his cohorts are interned
  And will, in turn, be fodder for an axe;
  Though I have noted well thy
  Legions lurking nigh the gate
  Which slates us for an impasse, so methink.

BILGEWATER
  Your majesties, if I might be so bold...

KING MILHOUS
  Dear Duke, was it not the boldness of thy stratagem
  That first sent Hameo hence and, shy of forethought,
  Roiled all our proles and lead me to this sorry state?
  Nay, I feel our further discourse must be
  'Mongst the sole fraternity of kings.
  Gentleman, if you will excuse us.

> [*Milhous and Bolingbras draw swords
> and stab Bilgewater and the Servant.*]

SERVANT
  Shall we die here, your majesty?

BOLINGBRAS
  Off yonder, if you please.

42. **smokéd from their holes:** After the 9/11 attacks, President George W. Bush vowed to find the terrorists responsible and "smoke them out of their holes." I believe Bush, in his heyday, was known to do more snorting than smoking but whatever floats your boat.

51. **abject liberty:** our country in a nutshell.

60. **schmo:** like a schmendrick, only yutzier

SERVANT
  This way, my lord.

  [*Exeunt the Servant and Bilgewater.*]

BOLINGBRAS
  As thou wast saying...

KING MILHOUS
  Firstly, of my forces be not phobic.
  For they shall to me e'er be nigh, should by the bye   40
  Some ruffians strike panic through the land
  And needs be smokéd from their holes
  And likewise set upon their soles.
  Or better still, some poor oppresséd people
  Crave a tyrant overthrown.   45
  So long as there's a beat within my chest
  Where blood shall course,
  And chests to fill with all their country's
  Wealth and natural resource,
  Those people shall be free   50
  And in good time be left to live abject liberty.

BOLINGBRAS
  Thy virtue brings unto mine eyes a tear.
  (Albeit that these weeps be laughter born.)

KING MILHOUS
  Do titter if thou must, dear Bolingbras.
  The only cause that keeps thy head unpiked   55
  Is that thy trifling treasuries urge not
  My aforementioned magnanimity.
  And thus, thy populace must suffer still.
  But let us to the case of Hameo.

BOLINGBRAS
  That vexsome schmo shall meet a sorry end.   60

KING MILHOUS
  Why yes, but when?
  Doth thy headsman hang on holiday?
  Need thee a carrot for thy garroter?
  Or prodding for thy squad of musketeers?

71. **the icing on his wake:** this usually precedes the frostin' on his coffin.

82-83. **blood-speckled banners...their graves:** O say can you see what I was going for there?

90. **Hameo is smoked...cured:** Does anyone else have a sudden craving for some nice, crispy bacon—or is that just me?

BOLINGBRAS
  Why this is queer.
  Should I not be the wiser, I wouldst fear
  Thou dost encourage his demise.

KING MILHOUS
  What part of "kill him" doth evade thy comprehension?

BOLINGBRAS
  Well if it is thy wish that it be so,
  And thou refuse to barter for his life,
  Thou'st robbed me of the icing on his wake.
  I now hath but one choice, for badness sake.
  I'll take me contrawise a counterstance
  And bid thee, friend, at my most firm behest,
  Not barter for his life, but now, his death.

KING MILHOUS
  You have my ear, dear Bolingbras.
  How have thee be the better by exchange?

BOLINGBRAS
  A war would serve us well in equal share.
  For patriotic clashes do best mask
  The raping of the paupered underclass,
  Whose last few ducats must be justly snatched
  So that blood-speckled banners may yet wave
  O'er the land of our greed and the home of their graves.

KING MILHOUS
  And whenst their final ducats have been drained,
  We'll each declare our victories
  And go on much the same.
  'Tis well enough, the game has oft been played.
  Now out with thy necessity to set us on our way.

BOLINGBRAS
  Once Hameo is smoked, thine ills are cured.
  His death will marshal military resolve.
  As well, my troops do need a rallying cry.
  A galvanizing spark to kindle spite.

107. **musketballs still fire on command:** It's what one might refer to as a *21-cum salute*.

108-09. **digit of a loving hand...prostatic rate:** otherwise known as "a pinky in the stinky."

118-20. **carnal drive...invalidate her parking:** this would be a car/sex metaphor—I couldn't resist. Would you turn away from it or yielded to temptation? The choices were manifold. My brain was on the rack; opinions steering me this way and that; but I tire of hearing them, in fact, I'm exhausted. I guess I'll deal with it later, somewhere down the road.

An act to turn their mere blood-like to lust.
Save this and our connivings shall go bust.

KING MILHOUS
Then put a name upon this evil and consider it as done. 95

BOLINGBRAS
Ensuring a most prosperitious slaughter
Necessitates that thou dost kill my daughter.

KING MILHOUS
Well that is low.
And thou art speaking to a man for whom
The gutter seems the heights of heaven. 100

BOLINGBRAS
Do not misconstrue, for I do love the lass,
But as woman, my Julinia's ill-suited as an heir.
Her death, while tragic, quickly fills my coffers
As described and untold wealth
Will pass unto my yet conceivéd son. 105
Yea, it can yet be done. I am still young.
My musketballs still fire on command—
Albeit aided by the digit of a loving hand.
And if finessed at just the right prostatic rate,
My people may yet greet 110
A freshly born new head of state.

KING MILHOUS
Well thanks for sharing.
But the prospect of this kindercide
Doth put me ill at ease.

BOLINGBRAS
Nay, 'tis but a breeze. 115
And to honey our alliance,
She's quite fetching to the eye.
With ne'er there yet a soul to take her carnal drive
Out for a spin. Perhaps, 'fore she subsides,
Thou might be pleased to invalidate her parking. 120

KING MILHOUS.
Thou art a most depraved and slimy eel. 'Tis a deal.

122. **Milly!:** Since this play takes place in 1512 AD, this king was certainly not a thoroughly modern Milly.

123. **Bolly!:** This became a nickname for the monarch after he traveled to India and founded the Hindi-language film industry.

137. **disbelief's abandoned willingly:** The term *a willing suspension of disbelief* was coined in 1817 by poet and philosopher Samuel Taylor Coleridge, who suggested that an audience or reader would suspend judgment of the implausibility of a story for the sake of entertainment. If you're having trouble with your suspension of disbelief, pop into your local Meineke for a tune-up.

BOLINGBRAS
  Milly!

KING MILHOUS
  Bolly!

                                              [*The kings embrace.*]

BOLINGBRAS
  In honor of our most egregious pact,
  Let's fly unto an eve of festival.   125
  There's food and wine and
  Winsome wenches at thy feet.
  And then, to the theatre. Ah, the theatre.
  Where for an instant's grace, the common man,
  As we, may flee the foolishness hubris of our leaders,   130
  The scowls of superiors, the grousing of our spouses
  And the din of our dear children for the things
  That we can surely ill afford, as we are underpaid
  And overtax and overwrought and underloved.
  For in the theatre, by the flicker of footlight's glow,   135
  An orchestra resounds most thrillingly
  And disbelief's abandoned willingly.
  Antagonized protagonists fulfill their fated arcs
  Or storied songs are coupled with the prancings
  Of some fancy girls (and nancy boys)   140
  So that we may enjoy brief respite from banal reality.

KING MILHOUS
  Sounds wonderful. Does it work?

BOLINGBRAS
  No, not really—but it is quite expensive.

KING MILHOUS
  Well, I hope we have good seats.

BOLINGBRAS
  Of course we have good seats;   145
  I have a friend at Will-Call.

                                              [*Exeunt.*]

A Bard's Day's Night
('s Dream)

ACT IV

4.1 Hameo and his company prepare for their royal performance. He warns the player not to use any discourteous language or racial slurs, and in doing so, using one himself. Top Dog takes offense at this slight but soon members of the audience complain that they have all experienced various racial indignities, feeling they too deserve special deference. Hameo drags the playwright on stage to answer for what is his scripted chaos.

8-9. **superfly...stick it to the king:** a reference to the film *Superfly*—the tagline for the movie being "He's got a plan to stick it to the man!"

27. **undulating cream holsters:** avoid if you are lactose intolerant

28. **flesh packed hinter satchels:** what four out of five anacondas prefer

ACT IV

4.1 *Enter Hameo, Julinia,*
Lymetrius and the Players.

HAMEO
  Now players, mark thee the re-workings of the plot.

SNOTRAG
  Whaddup with the rewrite, yo?

HAMEO
  The suspicions that I harbor of my uncle-king
  Will be set ablaze or laid to rest
  By condition of his bearings 5
  'Pon the viewing of our jest.

TOP DOG
  I diggest where thou comest from, my royal chum.
  Yo, check the rap that's writ here by my superfly.
  'Cause he's got a thing to stick it to the king.
  (*rapping*)

> *So let's knock it out fools* 10
> *And don't be pullin' your puds*
> *And we be seeing if that old emperor's*
> *Really wearing some duds. Shit.*

HAMEO
  Before we take the stage
  Do heed my fond admonishment; 15
  For I am privy to the less than
  Decorous lyrics ye do commonly recite,
  Which likely's why I found ye dungeon bound.
  Do note, this eve our show's for courtiers
  And courteous prevails. So hear me well, 20
  Emit ye not a peep or save thy final bows
  For rodents of the wretched castle-keep.
  We shall stay true to the tale as inked.
  Thou shalt couch all glib ad-libitums.
  Thou wilt withhold disparagement 25
  Of womankind, whether noting
  The allure of their undulating cream holsters
  Or the bulbosity of their flesh-packed hinter satchels.

32. **copulator of their progenitress:** motherfucker

35. **don't say n*****:** "Uttering this word is much worse than saying '*it*.'"—The Knights Who Say "Ni!"

Neither shall ye lionize nor coax
The slaying of our peacekeepers,
Nor shalt thou slight one as
A copulator of their progenitress,
Nor utter any other terms that may disturb
The delicate sensibilities of our patronage—
And whatever you do, don't say "nigger."

TOP DOG
What the f— Did he jus—? Did I hea—?
Did you just use the N-word?

HAMEO
Well, yes. I...I guess I did use the N-word.
But it was for illustrative purposes.

TOP DOG
I didn't ask why you used the N-word.
I don't care why you used the N-word.
You just can't use the N-word.
Now, I can use the N-word.
I can use the N-word anytime I want.
Check it, N-word, N-word, N-word.
See, just like that. Know why?
'Cause I am an N-word.
I'm an N-word from my inwards to my outwards.
And we N-words can use the N-word anytime we want.
But you ain't no N-word.
You ain't never gonna be no N-word.
So you ain't got no business using the N-word.

PUERTO RICAN IN AUDIENCE
You know, enough of this crap
Already about the fuckin' N-word.
You think black people are the only ones
Who can get offended? I'm Puerto Rican.
People call me spic all the time. I gotta deal with it.
Why everybody gotta tippy-toe around the black man?
You know what? From now on,
You wanna talk about me, you gotta use the S-word.
Haddaya like that?

68. **Niña, Pinta and that other ho:** that "other ho" being the Santa Maria, Christopher Columbus' flagship vessel on his voyage from Palos de la Frontera, Spain to the New World in 1492.

86. **tzuris:** (Yiddish) trouble; difficulty
87. **mishpocheh**: (Yiddish) family
88. **lokh in kop:** (Yiddish) hole in the head
89. **schtickl:** (Yiddish) a small amount; a bit of

ASIAN IN AUDIENCE
   Oh, no, no, no. Not so fast.
   We Asians got dibs on S-word.
   People always make fun of me. Way I drive. Way I talk.
   I no like they say slant to me. Very disrespect.   65
   We take S-word first. My culture go back 5000 year.
   People say we slant when you still sailing around
   On Niña, Pinta and that other ho.

PUERTO RICAN IN AUDIENCE
   You don't need no S-word.
   You can use the C-word for chink,   70
   The J-Word for jap and
   The G-word for gook.
   You see, you got it covered.

ASIAN IN AUDIENCE
   Oh. I no think of that. Not bad idea.
   We take one from column A, two from column B.   75
   OK-OK, you keep S-word.

IRISHMAN IN AUDIENCE
   Well, if we're all gonna be honest about it.
   I'm not too fond of all the mick calling, don't ya know.
   So I'll take the M-word for meself.
   And to save us a wee bit of time,   80
   The L-word for this limey bastard sitting next to me.

ENGLISHMAN IN AUDIENCE
   That's right, Governor. L-word suits us just fine.

IRISHMAN IN AUDIENCE
   And for the record,
   I've never been chasing after no Lucky Charms.
   If ya be asking me, they taste like shite.   85

JEW IN AUDIENCE
   Vell, I tell ya. I don't want to cause anybody any tzuris
   But on behalf of me and my mishpocheh,
   I need that kike talk like a lokh in kop.
   So we'll take the K-word on rye
   With a schtickl cream cheese.   90

93. **Got in himmel:** (Yiddish) God in heaven

94. **pupik:** belly button; **petselehs:** little penises

95. **meshuggeners:** foolish or crazy people

102. **Cor blimey:** euphemism for "God blind me."; **Jerry:** a nickname given to Germans by English soldiers because their helmets resembled English chamber pots, which in English slang were called "jerries."; **wanker:** a pejorative English term for a masturbater. **Note: a *Jerry wanker* is not related to the episode "The Contest" from the TV series *Seinfeld*.

107. **frog:** a pejorative term for the people of France, derived from either their penchant for eating frogs, living in a swampy land or their King Clovis wearing three toads on his shield and flag. But who really cares?—they're French.

GERMAN IN AUDIENCE
  You'll take the K-word?
  We Krauts will have the K-word.

JEW IN AUDIENCE
  Oy, Got in himmel.
  I've had it up to the pupik with these petselehs.
  You didn't take enough from us already?
  I don't understand these meshuggeners.
  Like my Uncle Schmuel used to say,
  "Everyone is kneaded out of the same dough
  But not baked in the same oven."

GERMAN IN AUDIENCE
  What oven would you like to be baked in?
  Perhaps I could arrange something.

ENGLISHMAN IN AUDIENCE
  Cor blimey, that's a low blow, you Jerry wanker.

GERMAN IN AUDIENCE
  Why are you all ganging up on me? All we did
  Was try to kill everyone and take over the world.
  How long you going to hold that over our heads?

FRENCHMAN IN AUDIENCE
  He is right. Leave the German along.
  And give us Frogs the F-word.

ENGLISHMAN IN AUDIENCE
  Oy, I got an F-word for ya all right.

HAMEO
  Enough!!

TOP DOG
  Yo, what you yellin 'bout?
  You the one that got this party started.

HAMEO
  Nay, although it would be seeming so, I, as are we all,
  Am but a hostage to this vulgar dramaturge.
  Now answer to thine impudence.

  Enter Playwright, dragged onstage by Hameo.

116. **the little man behind the curtain:** referring to the less than great and powerful professor masquerading as *The Wizard of Oz*.

132-33. **NIJ level IV anti-ballistic Kevlar vest:** The National Institute Justice (NIJ) tests body armor for law enforcement and the military. A Level IV vest can stop armor-piercing ordinance like a .30-06 Springfield M2 armor-piercing bullets at a velocity of 878 m/s ± 9.1 m/s.

138-39. **water resistant to three atmospheres:** mentioned as one of the selling points of the Rouchefoucauld watch Dan Ackroyd pawned in the film *Trading Places* (1983).

143-44. **"content of our character" thing:** "I look to a day when people will not be judged by the color of their skin, but by the content of their character."—Martin Luther King Jr. I couldn't not agree more with the sentiment from the late Dr. King. Unfortunately, the content of most people character these days is *fuuucked*!

147-48. **in perfect har-mo-ny:** referencing the lyrics "I'd like to teach the world to sing in perfect harmony" from a 1971 Coca-Cola commercial.

PLAYWRIGHT
  Alright, alright. So you want to hear from 115
  The little man behind the curtain? Fine.
  I'll take the mea culpa on this one. Thought you
  Could handle a little socio-political commentary
  Along with your entertainment. Eh, guess I was wrong.
  First off, I'd like to say to anyone who was insulted 120
  Here this evening and to all of the beaners, babaloos,
  Polacks, Ghandis, dagos, towelheads and others we
  Did not mention but were insulted in spirit,
  That I have in fact been duly authorized by special
  Arrangement with the United Nations, under 125
  Section 32b, article 5, subchapter c of the international
  Covenant on civil and political rights, for judicious
  Usage of the full and unexpurgated panglobal array
  Of racial epithets and slurs for educational and comedic
  Purposes. To those who still take umbrage with our 130
  Script and are given to acts violence, please note that
  I am wearing a field tested NIJ level IV anti-ballistic
  Kevlar vest with combination Dyneema and ceramic
  Plates which provide ample protect from projectiles
  Up to 9mm and most forms of fragmentation grenade 135
  Shrapnel. And for close encounters, a 3-milliamp Tazer
  Watch with electro-musclar disruption technology
  And a quartz movement which is water resistant to
  Three atmospheres. I just wanted to make the point that
  We all seem to be getting a little too sensitive about 140
  Our cultural backgrounds. And if we all would just
  Take a little more pride in ourselves as individuals,
  Not affiliates, get down with the whole "content of
  Our character" thing, scrap the polarizing and jam on
  The compromising, we could put some international 145
  And domestic body bag companies out of business—
  And then kickback, buy the world a Coke and live in
  Perfect har-mo-ny. Just a thought. I now return you to
  Your regularly schedule program, already in progress.

                [*The Cast applauds. Exit Playwright.*]

150-54. **All right...come back a star:** a play on the pep talk given by the director, Julian Marsh, in the backstage musical *42nd Street*.

157. **théâtre town:** using the French pronunciation of theater.

165: **customonious:** customary, usual or habitual; **immemmumified:** extending beyond the reach of memory.

166. **archeodiluvious:** of or relating to the period before the flood described in the Bible

167. **perambulatory extremity:** leg

170-73. **Scottish dude...we all gonna die!":** It is a superstition among theater performers that mentioning the play *Macbeth* before a performance brings bad luck. Reading the word "Macbeth" doesn't do anything so I think you're OK.

HAMEO
  All right, I'm through.
  Now keepest thee thy feet upon the ground
  And thy head upon thy shoulders, and go out,
  And players, you're going out some rapsters
  But you've got to come back a star...or we're all dead.
  Now let us take our places and good luck to one and all.

TOP DOG
  Yo, yo, yo, Hameo. 'Tis a rule unwrit
  Before the shit goes down in théâtre town,
  That the wishing of luck is gonna muck up the muck.
  And since we all doth know'st that our lives
  Be on the line, 'twould be superfine of thee
  To give some props to our theatric superstish
  And dish us some hurt as not to jinx-up the works.

HAMEO
  'Tis odd but I'll comply. What do you suggest of I?

TOP DOG
  Lay it out, Q-Tip.

Q-TIP
  'Tis customonious, from time immemumified
  To utilize the hereunder archeodiluvious phraseology,
  "Breakest thee, thy perambulatory extremity."

HAMEO
  OK. Break a leg. Canst we take our places now?

SNOTRAG
  Damn, next thing thou knowest,
  He gonna mention the Scottish dude.

HAMEO
  Thou cannot speak of Scots?
  Wait till my cousin Macbeth hears of this.

SNOTRAG
  Oh damn, now we all gonna die!!

4.2 Our heroes and the players perform a "rap" play for King Milhous and Bolingbras depicting the death of Hyperius as arranged by Milhous. The king is incensed, believing Bolingbras to be behind the affront and that Hameo, once revealed, is not dead as per their agreement. Milhous chases the players off with a sword. Bolingbras stabs Hameo for ruining his pact with Milhous. Julinia poisons herself over Hameo's death but he soon revives as his wound is not severe. The two lovers continue to ineffectually "kill" themselves over the other's demise until realizing they are both unharmed and they rejoice. Hameo asks for Julinia's hand but she is coyly reluctant.

Flourish: "Let go on with the show" from *There's No Business Like Show Business*.
5. **Elsinore:** the name of the castle in *Hamlet*.
8. **Birnam Wood:** a forest mentioned in *Macbeth*.
Player's Rap: *Parents Just Don't Understand* by DJ Jazzy Jeff & The Fresh Prince

4.2   *Trumpets sound. Enter Bolingbras,*
                  Milhous, Hippopotima and courtiers.

BOLINGBRAS
  Let the festivities begin.

                  Enter Schmuck.

SCHMUCK
  Good eve to thee, ladies and germs.
  Have we got a show for ye tonight.
  They rocked the House of Lords,
  They screamed for more at Elsinore, and now,   5
  From our dungeon hold with a tale to unfold,
  They cool, they dope, they Ethiops,
  The boys in the hood from Birnam Wood,
  Let's give a nice warm, Castle Bolingbras
  Welcome to...THE PLAYERS!!   10

            [The "Player's Rap" begins with a beautiful
                  tune that is both fresh and princely.]

TOP DOG
        Y'all sit right back
        'Cause I got for thee a yarn
        About a Queen and a King
        And his bro that done him harm
        'Cause he did covet his wife   15
        And he coveted the crown
        So he was coming up with a plan
        To bring the main man down.
        He say...

HAMEO
        Yo, yo, brother.   20
        Since I love thee like no other,
        I went out to arrange
        To get for thee a piece of strange.
        A mighty fine beeotch,
        I say the cream of the crotch.   25
        And what's more she is a rookie
        'Cause she never had no nookie.

30. **poon:** this "tang" is not the instant breakfast drink

34. **jiggy with her jelly:** this could probably mean whatever you want it to mean but it sounds like somebody's up to no good.

39. **the crib of ill-repute:** a brothel

52. **biddies:** little old ladies

55. **Don't wanna mess with no Tipper:** The Second Lady of the United States during the Clinton administration, Tipper Gore, petitioned Congress to add warning labels to music albums with explicit lyrics. She immediately became the darling of the hip-hop and rap community.

LYMETRIUS

> *Well, danke schoen,*
> *I hardly could abstain.*
> *To pass on poon like that*   30
> *I'd have to be insane.*
> *So put the bridge o'er the moat,*
> *I'll grab my crown and my coat*
> *Then I'll get jiggy with her jelly*
> *And that's all she wrote.*   35

TOP DOG

> *So the king and his little brother*
> *Started on their commute*
> *To get a piece of petoot*
> *At the crib of ill-repute.*
> *And when his majesty met the chick*   40
> *He started smackin' his lips*
> *'Cause she was everything*
> *That he dreamed of*
> *Plus a bag of chips.*
> *She say...*   45

JULINIA

> *Come on Kingy,*
> *Whip out yo mighty thingy.*
> *When I get you in the back,*
> *You'll have a happy sack.*

                                          [*Enter Playwright.*]

PLAYWRIGHT

> *I say, hold up, hold up,*   50
> *This be a family show.*
> *We don't want the biddies and the kiddies*
> *Up and hitting the do'.*
> *So just hang on to yo' zipper,*
> *Don't wanna mess with no Tipper.*   55

56-57. **I'm down with the FCC...you know me:** a reference to the Naughty by Nature song, "O.P.P."

58. **pervs in the hood:** As the old saying goes, "A perv in the hood is worth two in the bush"—which is probably where you'll find them.

66. **Our PG ratin':** with this song, as with the entirety of this play, parental guidance is suggested.

72. **Ahh, love to love you, baby:** always nice to be able to slip a little Donna Summer into the mix.

HASHPIPE

> *I'm down with the FCC.*

ALL

> *Yeah, you know me!*

SNOTRAG

> *To all the pervs in the hood*
> *Who want it nasty and good...*

HASHPIPE

> *We gotta be blocking* 60
> *All the knocking*
> *Like ya know we should.*

PLAYWRIGHT

> *Don't mean to switch what we baitin'.*
> *Now come on, don't be hatin',*
> *'Cause the brothers and me* 65
> *Has got to keeping our PG ratin'.*
> *Go!*

[*Exit Playwright.*]

[*Starvin' Marvin, Snotrag and Hashpipe block the view of this coupling.*]

JULINIA

> *Stick your royal wick into my thicket.*
> *Flog your dirty dog and tell 'em "sic it."*
> *Stick your royal wick into my thicket.* 70
> *Flog your dirty dog and tell 'em "sic it."*

LYMETRIUS

> *Ahh, love to love you, baby.*
> *Ahh, love to love you, baby.*

STARVIN' MARVIN (*taking a peek.*)
> *That's hot.*

JULINIA	LYMETRIUS	
Stick your royal wick	*Ahh,*	75
Into my thicket.		
Flog your dirty dog	*Love to love*	
And tell 'em "sic it."	*You, baby.*	

93. **You know my pippy is drippy:** Ask your doctor if Azithromycin is right for you.

100. **Tequila!:** If you haven't seen the comedy classic *Pee-wee's Big Adventure* (1985), you've miss the touching story of the bond shared between one special boy...and his bike. If you do catch a screening, be sure and tell them Large Marge sent ya.

	JULINIA	LYMETRIUS	
	Stick your royal wick	*Ahh,*	
	Into my thicket.		80
	Flog your dirty dog	*Love to love*	
	And tell 'em "sic it."	*You, baby.*	

TOP DOG

    So when the king was through,
    His royal scepter withdrew.
    And to the skank he gave his thanks   85
    And bid a fond adieu.
    But in a couple of weeks
    He wasn't feelin' up to peak
    And so he called for the doc
    Who ask him...   90

SNUGGY BEAR

    Whaddup, G?

LYMETRIUS

    Somethin' wrong downtown.
    Ya know my pippy is drippy.
    To be givin' it to ya straight
    I feel my shape ain't too shippy.   95
    In regard to my boys,
    I hardly can feel ya,
    And my worm feel like it's squirmin'
    In a bottle o'...

ALL

    Tequila! (dance break.)   100

TOP DOG

    He took a look in his jock
    And then the doc say...

SNUGGY BEAR

    Yo,
    My assessin' is you messin'
    With a ghonorous ho.   105

TOP DOG

    He gave 'im potions and lotions

115. **homie:** homeboy or male friend that comes from your home town. (This slang term is generally traced to Mexican-American Spanglish and some etymologists have said the term *homeboy* may be derived from the Spanish word *hombre* which means *man*. The term was also popularized by Damon Wayans on the television show, *In Living Color* with his portrayal of an ex-con named, Homey D. Clown, known to not "play that.")

122. **coinky dinky:** an adorable way of saying the word *coincidence*

ALL
> *But they no damn good.*

TOP DOG
> *The king would soon*
> *Be having to rule*
> *A subterranean hood.* 110
> *He say...*

LYMETRIUS
> *It look like the end.*
> *Where be my brother, my friend?*

TOP DOG
> *He say...*

HAMEO
> *You know, I ain't thy homie.* 115
> *That was all pretend.*

TOP DOG
> *So from the syph and the strife*
> *You know...*

ALL
> *The old king croaked.*

TOP DOG
> *And his bro took crown and queen* 120
> *'Cause he the meanest of folks.*
> *So if ya see coinky dinky*
> *In the tale that we do.*
> *It really shouldn't be no surprise*

ALL
> *Because we talkin' 'bout...* 125

KING MILHOUS
Wait!
For I can no more tolerate this slur.
Thou think thee clever, do thee Bolingbras,
To put the looking glass before mine eyes
And have my conscience bear this graphic foe? 130

BOLINGBRAS
But I, as thee, am equally aghast
And vow this cast of scoundrels will atone
As they are flayed to bone for insolence.

139. **something stinks in Denmark:** referring to the line, "Something is rotten in the state of Denmark" from Shakespeare's *Hamlet*.

145. **A literal left wing conspiracy:** The right and left parts of the stage that are not visible to the audience are called *wings*—so was a pretty shitty band formed by Paul McCartney (even he said so).

152. **What you talkin' 'bout, Milhous?:** It takes *Diff'rent Strokes* to change the world.

KING MILHOUS
Which slanderer concocted this offense?

HAMEO
Why look, 'tis I, thy nephew, Hameo. 135
I jettison my mask for thee to see,
As thy mask too hast slipped clear of its place
For all to spy the vile double face of fratricide.
I must confide, something stinks in Denmark.

SCHMUCK (*hand fanning behind.*)
No, actually that was me. Sorry. 140

KING MILHOUS
So Bolingbras, thou dost decry this sly skullduggery?
Then wherefore doth my brother's son run free?
Methought him captive of thy dungeon hold.
Not here upon the stage to boldly wage
A literal left wing conspiracy. 145
The war thou sought in pretense
Will commence, my friend, in earnest.
And now I shall in turn convoke my legions
So that you, and this boy too, shall well be taught—
'Tis ne'er wise to inflame and risk my temper. 150
Sic semper tyrannis!

SNOTRAG
What you talkin' 'bout, Milhous?

KING MILHOUS
It's Latin for "thus always to tyrants."

SNOTRAG
Yeah, but ain't you a tyrant?

KING MILHOUS
No, damn it, I'm a despot. There's a big difference. 155

HASHPIPE (*taking a toke.*)
Like I always say, "Despot is the best pot."

KING MILHOUS
Die ruffians!!!!

169. **the boatman beckons me:** In many cultures, it was believed that a guide transported the dead by boat to their final destination. In Greek mythology, he was named Charon. A coin was required as payment for this perilous journey but in recent years, Charon began accepting Metrocard.

And, lo! toward us in a bark
Comes on an old man, hoary white with eld,
Crying, " Woe to you, wicked spirits!"

Canto III., lines 70-72.

*[King Milhous chases Lymetrius and
the Players with a sword. Exeunt.]*

BOLINGBRAS
My selfsame sentiment to thee, young Hameo.
Thou hast muddled my alliance with the king...

[Bolingbras removes Julinia's mask.]

And turned my very blood against her maker. 160
Now take my dagger as thy recompense. (*stabs Hameo.*)
Would I the time to see thine anguished twist
And multiply the sting a thousand fold,
But war me now awaits.
And so to ready, I must get me hence. 165

[Wounded, Hameo falls.]
[Exeunt Bolingbras and Courtiers.]

HIPPOPOTIMA
My lady, praise to heaven, thou art safe.

JULINIA
Nay, dear maid, for I am slain in empathy
As Hameo's most precious embers fade.

HAMEO
Julinia, the boatman beckons me.
But I shall wait for thee upon the shores of doom, 170
Beneath the weeping palms, at life-death's brink.
I'll be the one who holds aloft a fruity drink
With one of those little paper umbrellas sticking out of it.
Ya really can't miss me.

[Hameo dies.]

JULINIA
Puck, exert thy wizardry 175
And wrench him from the reaper's grasp.

SCHMUCK
Alas, I have no sway beyond our earthly realm.

190. **'Tis in my pants:** Pucks are horny little creatures, aren't they?

195. **bandicoot:** It's Australian for *rat*, mate!

196. **expectorant:** helps loosen mucus when you least expect it.

201. **drama queen:** every woman you've ever known.

JULINIA
   Then I shall take the helm
   And guide my poor ephemeral vessel
   Out beyond these mortal waves
   And come to rest upon that blissful shoal.
   And now I say to thee, sweet poisoned flask,
   Do have me set a sail as I have asked.

   [Julinia drinks and dies.]

SCHMUCK
   What the fuck!?!

HIPPOPOTIMA
   She cast aside her days for Hameo.
   Ah, how delicious.

SCHMUCK
   Where is thy mind? She's dead!
   Ne'er I to comprehend of womankind.
   There's nowhere they can fail to find romance.
   Yet hold, save one—'tis in my pants.
   Where came she by this flask of rapid death?

HIPPOPOTIMA
   Julinia is e'er to have one near.
   For who can say when circumstance should deem
   That life, too grave, give way to endless dream.
   But fear thee not, my nerve-racked bandicoot.
   Imbibed she but a mild expectorant.
   And I suspect she'll soon rise from her swoon
   And walk it off without a cough.
   These histrionics far to oft I've seen.
   O yea, she is a princess
   But in faith, a drama queen.

SCHMUCK
   Then as she sleeps, I'll tend to Hameo.
   For duty bound am I, his woodland squire,
   To now convey his noble frame
   And rest it 'pon the pyre.

208. **yachting with the tillerman:** not a reference to Charon the ferryman but rather the exciting follow-up album to *Tea for the Tillerman* by Cat Stevens

213. **this lesser therebefore:** Come on, America. Let's make this lesser therebefore great again!

224. **follow suit:** to do the same as someone else (This is derived from card games in which one would play a card of the same suit as the player before; also, in a situation in which some guy shows up wearing a really nice suit —perhaps an Armani or Hugh Boss— you would listen to him, believe everything he said, and perhaps, literally follow him because, again, *nice suit*.)

229. **to end me with a tug:** This tug doesn't sound like it lead to a happy ending.

[*He tries to lift Hameo.*]

HAMEO (*revived.*)
Ahhh! Ya hoofed me in the balls.

SCHMUCK
Do pardon me, my liege.
We thought thee yachting with the tillerman.

HAMEO
I glimpsed him for a wisp of time.
But as mine eyes were penniless, 210
I could but ill-afford the fare
And so from Charon's gate was rudely flung,
Right from that great hereafter to this lesser therebefore.

SCHMUCK
Death and taxes. Whaddya gonna do?
Now by-your-leave, I'll minister thy wound. 215
I say, the barb of Bolingbras
Left no more than a whisker nick.

HAMEO
Unclaw me, Schmuck.
What happenings befell Julinia?
O, 'tis unmissable. This tainted flask 220
Within her gentle grasp divulges all.
My now undone demise
Did grieve her toward life's forfeiture.
Then I shall follow suit and fold my hand.
For I can do no less for thee, my love. 225

SCHMUCK
But Hameo...

HAMEO
Dissuade me not, my furry friend.
I'll fashion from this belt a hangman's loop
And cinch it snug to end me with a tug. Ahhh...

[*Hameo dies.*]

231. **Methinks Julinia bestirs herself:** When I bestir myself, I try to keep a box of tissues close at hand.

236. **hempen strands:** This hemp is rope and will not give you a case of the munchies.

244. **take the savage ball:** Too many options here. I guess I'll just leave this one alone.

248. **A flash within the pan:** something which disappoints after a promising beginning, e.g., gunpowder flashing without a bullet being fired (Also, if you cum too quickly while fucking Peter Pan.)

SCHMUCK
  Well that's just great. 230

HIPPOPOTIMA
  Methinks Julinia bestirs herself.

JULINIA
  What clamorous commotion brought me forth?

SCHMUCK
  Thy paramour regained vitality,
  But at the bitter sight of thee expired,
  Did reaquire death by his own hand 235
  With nothing more than will and hempen strands.

JULINIA
  Who couldst divine my vain theatrics
  Wouldst engender such a pretty pass?

SCHMUCK
  The fact that thy theatrics are in vain
  By now is quite apparent to us all. 240

JULINIA
  (*Aside.*) Now that's cold. (*to Schmuck.*)
  Then I shall now in earnest join the dust.
  I'll snatch this rusty musket from the wall
  And ope my lips to take the savage ball.

SCHMUCK
  Julinia, No!!!! 245
                    [*Julinia fires the weapon and dies.*]

HIPPOPOTIMA
  Those firearms are solely powder primed.
  My lady just fell faint from the report.

SCHMUCK
  A flash within the pan...as are we all.

HAMEO (*revived.*)
  My ears do ring recountings of a shot.

SCHMUCK
  Back so soon, my lord? 250

257. **Should ticket thee for flights of angels:** a reference to the line, "And flights of angels sing thee to thy rest" spoken upon the death of the famed prince in *Hamlet* (If you're an angel looking to get out of town for the weekend, the best prices for flights can be found on Cherubosity.com)

258-60. **O, you too, too solid rock...happy dagger?:** these are plays on other Shakespeare lines from *Hamlet* and *Romeo & Juliet*—also from the popular children's game of the 16th century, "Rock, Papyrus, Dagger."

HAMEO
The dying left my brawn bereft of strength
To kept the neck-knot taut suffice for death.

SCHMUCK
Bummer.

HAMEO
O, thou sarcastic satyr,
Aid me now to consummate my lethal task. 255

SCHMUCK
As you so command. A stone's blow to the cranium
Should ticket thee for flights of angels.

HAMEO (*Smashing the stone into his head.*)
O, you too, too solid rock.

                    [*Hameo dies as Julinia revives.*]

SCHMUCK
Next!

JULINIA
Doest thou have a happy dagger? 260

SCHMUCK
Oh, let's see. Uh...this one's a little out of sorts.
This one's copacetic but I think we can do
Better than that. Got a metso-metso, a hunky-dory.
This one's manic-depressive, I don't really think you
Wanna go there. Ah, here we go. One happy dagger... 265

JULINIA (*dramatically.*)
O...

SCHMUCK
To rust within thy sheath.

JULINIA
You had to kill the moment, didn't ya?

                    [*Julinia stabs herself and dies.*]

SCHMUCK
Of course, rubber doesn't really rust that much, does it?

276-77. a gander at the gun...golden goose: "What's sauce for the goose is sauce for the gander" will no doubt be pretty irrelevant, at least for the particular geese in question, since it sounds like they're sitting in a pot somewhere about to be eaten. I would imagine the significance of the equality they were able to achieve, while heartwarming, will most probably be lost on them.

HAMEO (*revives.*)
  Is this the afterworld?

SCHMUCK
  Not yet, my liege. Do fancy thee to take another whack?

HAMEO
  Nay, my head is killing me.
  (And mocks that nought else here would seem to be.)

SCHMUCK
  This musket shall propel thee to the void.
  The very one Julinia employed, a mere two deaths ago.

HAMEO
  Yea, taketh I a gander at the gun.
  The one to slay my lovely golden goose.
  And so I say farewell to thee, dear puck.
  With any luck, 'twill better stone and noose.

> [*Julinia revives. Hameo pulls the trigger, nothing happens.*]

JULINIA
  That weapon there can be a wee bit tricky,
  First you have to pull back this doohickey.

HAMEO
  Oh, thanks.

> [*Hameo cocks the gun and puts it to his head, then...*]

  Julinia!!

JULINIA
  Oh Hameo!!!

> [*Hameo and Julinia embrace.*]

SCHMUCK
  Hippopotima!

> [*Opens arms for an embrace, gets nothing.*]

  Hippopotima!

> [*Hippopotima, unenthused, scratches Schmuck behind his ear.*]

302. **Is you is or is you ain't my baby?:** from the title of the 1943 Louis Jordan hit (The original title, "Be You Am or Ain't You Were My Girlfriend?," was changed by the record label shortly after release.)

4.3 Kings Milhous and Bolingbras command their armies to attack each other. Unfortunately, these armies consist only of Rosenstern and Guildencrantz, who charge at each other with spears and are both slain. Bolingbras, seeing Hameo still alive, launches into a sword fight with him in which the king is defeated and dies.

SCHMUCK (*one leg twitching.*)
  Oww-that's-good-right-there-yeah.

HAMEO
  My fair Julinia,
  We have traversed the existential fjords,
  Defiant of the edicts nature fixed   290
  So that we evermore may be as one.
  Praise heaven for this miracle bestowed
  For which eternal gratitude is owed.
  So when shall we be wed, my glowing bride?

JULINIA
  Do we really have to decide all that right now?   295
  I mean, maybe we should date for a little while,
  See how things go?

HAMEO
  Thou heretofore hast offered up thy life
  For lack of mine and now irresolute to wife me?
  Well I am not so given to caprice.   300
  Now answer this and say not maybe.
  Is you is or is you ain't my baby?

              [*Flourish: after Louis Jordan's "baby."*]

HIPPOPOTIMA
  The king approaches.

4.3   *Enter King Milhous and Rosenstern.*

KING MILHOUS
  Bolingbras, show thyself, thou foul scoundrel.

              Enter Bolingbras and Guildencrantz.

  As has been sworn and promiséd, returned have I to take
  Thy castle and thy foolish head.

BOLINGBRAS
  You and what army?

KING MILHOUS
  Thy barricades are breached,   5
  And but a moment hence my regulars,
  A thousand strong, will storm this fortress hold.

10. **loopholes:** small slits in castle walls that allowed archers to fire arrows and remain protected (Today we used them to get out of paying taxes.)

27. **Saint Crispin's Day:** recalling the rousing battle speech given by the king in Shakespeare's *Henry V* (This has nothing to do with Crispin Glover, who played George McFly in the movie *Back to the Future* (1985). He may at some point have been declared insane, but to the best of my knowledge, was never declared a Saint.)

ROSENSTERN
Ummm...I'm afraid that's not going to happen, sire.

KING MILHOUS
With torch aloft,
I hailed our forces from the loopholes.
An ocean of reserves are hither bound.

ROSENSTERN
Actually, that was just me, your majesty.

KING MILHOUS
How be it so?

ROSENSTERN
Perchance thou missed the signage at the sills.

KING MILHOUS (*reading.*)
"Armies in the castle window may be
Smaller than they appear."

BOLINGBRAS
By the bye, where is mine own battalion's hellish cry?

GUILDENCRANTZ
AHHHHHH!! Seems I'm it, your royalness.
Excess of sixty thousand straws we drew,
And lucky me, I'm here of them in lieu.
What you might call a bit of a skeleton crew.

KING MILHOUS
Well Bolingbras, 'twould seem
We have deserters in our midst.

BOLINGBRAS
(Or rather, not in our midst.)

GUILDENCRANTZ
Your highnesses, perhaps you may recall,
This day all grunts take respite from the brawl.
You know, it being Saint Crispin's Day and all.

ROSENSTERN
Perhaps, sire, if I may, 'tis best to stay
This battle royal till our other blokes are back.

49. **A visiting mother-in-law:** This particular curse is widely considered to be the most horrendous curse imaginable and reserved solely for the most heinous of enemies as a visiting mother-in-law has be known to cause grown men to cry in frustration and mental anguish—depending on the length of the visit.

KING MILHOUS
We will attack at once. Men...

ROSENSTERN
Man.

KING MILHOUS
Man. Ready armaments.

BOLINGBRAS
Prepare for engagement.

GUILDENCRANTZ
Your highness, for the love of Mike...

KING MILHOUS/BOLINGBRAS
CHARGE!!!

ROSENSTERN
Oh, bloody hell.

[*Rosenstern and Guildencrantz, with spears, charge and run each other through.*]

ROSENSTERN/GUILDENCRANTZ
Zounds!!!!

[*They fall over, dead.*]

HAMEO
O, what a senseless dismal sight.
Rosencrantz and Guildenstern are dead!

GUILDENCRANTZ
It's Guggenheim. (*dies.*)

ROSENSTERN
And Rubenfeld. (*dies.*)
But my friends call me Harvey. (*dies again.*)

HAMEO
How quickly do these monarchs rend their pawns?
Nor pay no higher homage to a prince
Or more so still unto his father-king.
Should ambition be but baffled
Let the snag be laid to waste.
I now impose the utmost curse for this disgrace.
A visiting mother-in-law on both your houses.

50. **raging bull:** a brief tribute to DeNiro/Scorsese.

61-64. **from miles off...pesty nat:** Since this is to be a "Jazz Duel," I chose to pay tribute to some of the legendary performers of the genre: Miles Davis, Charlie Parker (nicknamed "Bird"), Cab Calloway, Louis Armstrong (nicknamed "Satchmo"), Dizzy Gillespie, Duke Ellington and Nat King Cole.

66. **The king has left the building:** The king of rock and roll is dead. Long live King Elvis.

BOLINGBRAS
  This raging bull survived my picador. 50
  Yet soon will taste my saber's coup de grâce.

HAMEO
  Let this fiesta brava now commence.

JULINIA
  O Hameo, I pray do gore thee not this matador.
  Despite misdeed, he is a father well adored.

HAMEO
  Julinia, he let thee languish in the hold. 55

KING MILHOUS
  And bade me take thy life and revel in thy tender flesh—
  Though thou not yet be legal tender.

JULINIA
  Unto this horrid charge what can I say, save
  "Toro, Ole!"

BOLINGBRAS
  Presume to slander me without account? 60
  Fly hither, thee, from miles off, like bird on holiday
  And swoop down in this callow way
  To ope thy satchelmouth and drive my daughter dizzy?
  Well, raise thy weaponed duke thou pesky nat,
  As I go not for all that jazz. 65

                [*Bolingbras and Hameo draw swords and
                       duel to the theme from "Mannix."
                          Bolingbras is pierced and dies.*]

SCHMUCK
  The king has left the building. Thank you very much.

4.4 Schmuck's friend, the muskrat, arrives and reports that all are on their way after hearing of the conflict between their kings. Milhous abdicates his throne after he is confronted with his injustices. Hameo and Julinia agree to wed, with Lymetrius and his nostril hair also choosing to espousing themselves in the same nuptial ceremony.

4.4 *Enter Muskrat.*

SCHMUCK
Why, 'tis my little muskrat friend.
What matters brought thee hither?

MUSKRAT
Eek, eek-eek, eek-eek, eek.

HAMEO
What did he say?

MUSKRAT
I said "Eek!" Whaddareya, fuckin' deaf? 5

SCHMUCK
'Twould seem the countryside was set abuzz
By word of this upheaval in our realm.
And all are on the way to sate aroused curiosities
And mark whom shall obtain prevailing sovereignty.
'Sides, we're about two and a half hours into this shindig 10
And the sooner everybody shows,
The sooner we can ties up all the loose ends
And put this puppy to bed.

Enter Two and a Half Witches.

ALL WITCHES
We've traveled far on foot and knee
As premonitions come to be 15
And split the air with cackling laughs
We weathered witches two and a half.

HALF WITCH (*to Hameo.*)
Like that one? Wrote it myself. (*to Milhous.*)
Say...I know you. You're the bastard that took my legs.

FIRST WITCH
She foretold of his undoing. 20
That his reign wouldst be o'erthrown.

SECOND WITCH
And for this candid presage was injuriously delegged.

23. **misconstrue:** to interpret wrongly; a contestant in the Miss Universe pageant from the independent Polynesian island nation of Construe.

29. **untoward:** unseemly, improper or uncouth—basically everything you've read in the play thus far.

36. **Beheading, Beheading:** It was convention in medieval times to sing songs during an execution to raise the spirits of the condemned convict. This resulted in many popular hits of the day like *Chop Around the Block*, *Axes Keep Fallin' on My Head* and *It Was Decapitation, I Know*.

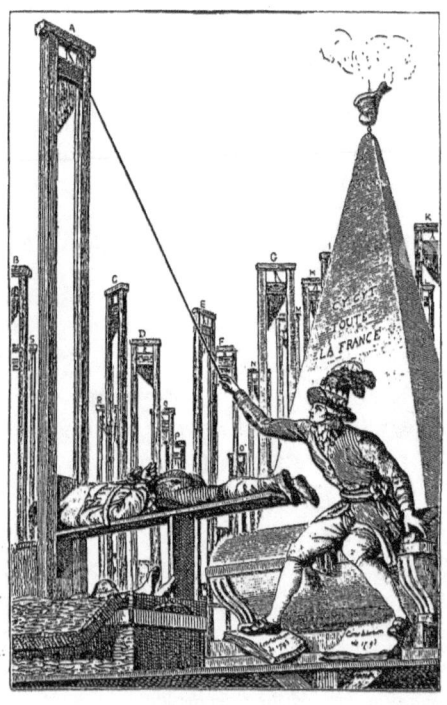

KING MILHOUS
  Methinks thou misconstrues me for another.
  Now if ye will excuse, I think I hear
  My mommy calling. Mommy?

Enter the Players.

STARVIN' MARVIN
  Y'all don't need yo mama. Thou gottest some
  Bad mothers right here, boyee.

TOP DOG
  Now weren't thou be the very kingly G
  That found our allegoric play untoward
  And thus pursued my black ass with a sword?

JULINIA
  'Twas assuredly no other that didst
  Trifle with my life and virtue.

HAMEO
  Or slew a noble sibling for ascension to his throne.

HALF WITCH
  Let me at 'im! I'll misconstrue my stump right up his ass.

SNOTRAG
  Seem to me this head be begging for the block.

SCHMUCK (*sings.*)

> *Beheading, Beheading,*
> *An end you should be dreading.*
> *One chop with force*
> *Will mean the divorce*
> *Of neck and shoulder's wedding.*
> *Your head will hit the bucket*
> *And bod'll twitch with fits.*
> *It's...a...behea...*

HAMEO
  Shut the puck up! We are not barbarians.
  We shall afford this king a courtesy,
  Despite his lack to grace us with the same.
  The floor is thine your highness,
  Thou may now defend thy name.

49-79. **My fellow countrymen...noon tomorrow:** On September 23rd, 1952, Richard Nixon, accused of receiving improper campaign donations, went on television to give his famous "Checkers" speech, named for the Cocker Spaniel he received from a supporter and said he would keep, after stating all other gifts received were used to defer political expenses. On August 8th, 1974, Nixon delivered his resignation address after a lengthy investigation revealed his cover-up of the break-in at the Democratic National Committee headquarters at the Watergate office complex in Washington, D.C. (Just think of the nightmare the whole country could have avoided if we weren't such suckers for cute little dogs.)

KING MILHOUS
  My fellow countrymen. I speakest to you tonight
  As a monarch whose honesty and integrity hath been
  Questionéd. Well, I bid welcome to this kind of
  Examination, because plebs have got to knoweth
  Whether or not their king is a tyrant. Well I'm not a
  Tyrant. I killed for, uh, earned everything I got. 'Tis
  True, I made a lot of ducats in the practice of raping and
  Pillaging the masses, and I claim not I was worth it,
  But what can I say? When the thumb-screw knobs
  Art turnéd tight, villagers do tend to render unto Caesar
  What is Caesars...and I worked pretty hard. And if
  The Duke of Bilgewater were alive today, he wouldst
  Hath confirméd that—right up until the moment
  I killed him. Now, that's not Milhous speaking, as I
  Fear not to have an independent source confirmth
  The facts, posthumously or otherwise. Now I knowest
  Ye may find this hard to believe, but I was once
  Belovéd in this land. I can recall after my coronation,
  A peasant who I tortured for back-taxes sent me a
  Present for my generosity (as I had left him three
  Fingers on one hand). 'Twas a little Welsh Terrier, black
  And white, stripéd, and we named him Backgammon.
  And I just want to say this right now, regardless of
  What they say about it, I'm gonna kill that dog.
  Now it doth appear ye wouldst have me shown the
  Door, preferring Hameo to rule and not have ol'
  Milhous to kick around anymore. Well, let me make
  One thing perfectly clear, I've never been a quitter,
  But, as head of state, prefer my head right where it be,
  Therefore I shall resigneth the monarchy, effective at
  Noon tomorrow.

MUSKRAT
  Why don't you just get the fuck out now?
  Do us all a favor.

KING MILHOUS
  Well, aren't you one rude little beaver.

86. **Come here, musky! I'll bust your hump:** In the presidential election of 1968, Richard Nixon was opposed by the Democratic nominee for vice president, Edmund Muskie and presidential nominee Hubert Humphrey.

99-100. **"Whenst one assumeth...you and me...eth.":** from a line by Tony Randall as Felix Unger on the classic television show, *The Odd Couple*.

MUSKRAT
  I'm a muskrat ya son of a bitch.

KING MILHOUS
  Why you little...

MUSKRAT
  Bring it on, tough guy.   85

KING MILHOUS
  Come here, musky! I'll bust your hump!

> [*King Milhous and the Muskrat
> brawl on the ground.*]

Enter Queen Patsy and Thelonious with Lobster.

THELONIOUS
  Lymetrius! Hameo! We came as soon as we...
  Why look, Lobster. 'Tis a muskrat beating forth
  The shit from a king. Well, ya don't see that everyday.

QUEEN PATSY (*separating the combatants.*)
  Cease this savagery at once! O, Hameo.   90
  I've heard such horrid tales whilst here en route.
  Of thy travails and of this man to whom I've wed.

HAMEO
  Queen mother dear, I pray, cast off thy dread.
  For yet again will all be well once do
  Assumeth I the throne.   95

THELONIOUS
  Take care, Prince Hameo. For as the sage hath said,
  "Whenst one assumeth,"... (*aside*) That's right,
  I'm gonna say it... (*to Hameo.*)
  "Whenst one assumeth, one doth make an ass
  Out of you and me...eth."   100

HAMEO
  Someone has got to get this man some help.
  And as for thee, thou counterfeited king,
  Thou art banishéd.

108. **Banishéd...joke...not...working...:** How many jokes in this play aren't working? You decide!

113. **Annnnnnd loving it:** If you know this tagline of Don Adams as Agent 86 in the '60s Mel Brooks TV comedy, *Get Smart*, I'm afraid you were born in the wrong era. ("Missed it by *that much*.")

ABRAHAM RENVOYANT AGAR

KING MILHOUS
  Banishéd? I am banishéd?

THELONIOUS
  That's funny. He looks more like Milhous to me. 105
  (*Aside.*) What? Nothing on that one? Well, ya know,
  We're still workshopping it. (*writing note.*)
  Banishéd...joke...not...working...

QUEEN PATSY (*to Milhous.*)
  Thou gave unto my dear Hyperius the prefix "late."
  And for my son didst scheme the selfsame fate. 110
  And now, for all thine ills, we're banishéd?
  Boy, art thou to get a really good working over tonight.

KING MILHOUS
  Annnnnnd loving it.
                                    [*Patsy hits Milhous.*]
  Ooo, Owww, Ooch!

HAMEO
  But mother, thou needs no more 115
  Be yoked with this pariah.

QUEEN PATSY
  Oh Hameo, cast off thy rash naiveté. You know
  How hard it is to find a man at my age? Sheesh.
  Besides, should sufferance be thy punitive intent,
  What greater torment more so couldst thou laud 120
  Than life abreast a bellyaching broad.

HAMEO
  Now sweet Julinia, once more do I implore.
  Wouldst thou not replicate this sentiment,
  Lay waste to my contentment,
  Withhold thy favors on a whim, 125
  Catalogue my foibles, create for me a world of strife,
  And deign to be my wife?

HIPPOPOTIMA
  Julinia, he is young and fair, of nimble wit and noble
  Birth, with land and wealth, and soon the rank and
  Dwellings of a king—and thou as well dost love him. 130

135. **get thee to a therapist:** In Shakespeare's *Hamlet*, the Prince of Denmark bade Ophelia "get thee to a nunnery." Oddly, nuns of the day were known to be the best source for psychoanalysis—with very attractive hourly rates.

144-45. **I'd prefer to keep my pants on:** Oh, that Thelonious. He's incorrigible.

146. **As you like it:** Now where did that line come from I wonder?

150. **mazel tov, my son:** Queen Patsy's maiden name was Horowitz.

JULINIA
  'Tis true, but is he really "the one?" I mean,
  What are his prospects? I always thought I could do
  So much better than this. What if I say "yes" and then
  Mr. Right comes along?

HIPPOPOTIMA
  Milady, get thee to a therapist.   135

JULINIA (*to Hameo.*)
  Unto thy tender wishes I comply.
  I proffer thee my hand, my heart, and
  All my aphrodital parts in matrimony
  And freely join thee as thy loving bride.

HAMEO
  If thou speak sooth then let us to the task.   140
  Prepare ye, one and all, to bask within our love
  As we are wedded here this day.
  And honored friends, I pray ye all bear witness.

THELONIOUS
  Well, if 'tis all the same to thee, I'd prefer to
  Keep my pants on, thank you very much.   145

HAMEO
  As you like it.
  Dear mother, I shall soften for thy sake
  And stay thy mate's eviction but a day,
  That thou might of our revelry partake.

QUEEN PATSY
  My thanks and love, and mazel tov, my son.   150
  But if I may presume to be so bold,
  Wouldst not this day, years hence in reverie,
  Be recollected far more pleasantly
  Were three decaying carcasses
  Not strewn upon the ground, allowing to confound   155
  The dearest memory of thy tender lives
  With that of rotting flesh and buzzing flies?
  Uh, just a thought.

162. **smoke these bones...drag:** If you need someone to smoke some bones, you could do no better than Hashpipe.

163-64. **"achtung." Mine hair:** A little something for the Germans in the audience. Holocaust schmolocaust, enjoy yourselves!

170. **bouncin' and behavin':** the tagline from the '80s Pert shampoo commercials—'cause if your hair doesn't bounce and behave why bother getting out of bed in the morning? (Kudos to the ad agency involved for honoring the old adage "Nothing moves product like a woman on a trampoline.")

171-77. **all is ducky...Earl of Sandwich:** Sounds like someone's getting hungry again.

HAMEO
  Kind players, wouldst thou serve me in this deed
  And prithee carry off this carrion? 160

TOP DOG
  Why yo, my prince, we'll do't and shall not lag.

HASHPIPE
  We'll smoke these bones and take 'em for a drag.

  [*Exeunt the Players carrying the bodies.*]

LYMETRIUS
  Good people, to thee all I cry "achtung."
  Mine hair and I fair tiding wouldst declare.
  This joyous day shall now be doubly so. 165
  For whilst she didst in jest at first quoth "no,"
  My little tease, in time, didst acquiesce
  And thus appeased my heart's perfervid plea.
  I'll groom my little raven, as for she,
  My bouncin' and behavin' bride will be. 170

HIPPOPOTIMA (*to Julinia.*)
  Sure, all is ducky for Lymetrius.
  He is to bread that o, so saucy wench, that raisin hussy.
  O, but what of me? Ne'er shall I meat a butter man
  Than he. That devildog's betrothal's all l'oranged
  And here ice cream, dear Lard, it were not so. 175
  What should I say then? Ca-sserole, 'sserole?
  Oh, where's the fuckin' Earl of Sandwich
  When ya need him?

HAMEO
  Lymetrius,
  I'd have not thy jocundity undone 180
  Or hampered by thy dirty linen aired.
  But as thou art my kin, in terms of heart,
  I fairly must impart to thee my mind.
  Breathe words, not I, against this curlicued
  Miss-tress to whom thou yearn to braid thy life, 185
  But know thou wert hairbrainéd by the puck
  And thy desire was enchantment spawned.

190-192. **my sly come-hither hair...It's witchcraft:** a classic from the chairman of the board, Frank Sinatra. *Witchcraft* (1957) composed by Cy Coleman with lyrics by Carolyn Leigh

193. **So shines...weary world:** mash-up of a line from *The Merchant of Venice* and Gene Wilder's Willy Wonka—give or take "a good deed," a "naughty," and a "weary."

200. **state of red**: It's like a state of denial—only with no gays or abortions.

202. **If love be the food of music, right on!:** a play on the line from Shakespeare's *Twelfth Night*.

216. **Now here's a hitch, the lady vanishes:** a reference to the classic 1938 Hitchcock film.

LYMETRIUS
Do tell what love was not begat the same?
By magic, moonbeam, alchemy of brain, it matters not.
A fragrance in the air or my sly come-hither hair... 190

HALF WITCH (*singing.*)
That strips my conscience bare.
It's witchcraft. Da-da, da da-da...sorry.

LYMETRIUS
So shines true love in such a weary world.
O, wouldst thou have me yield my interest
And peradventure ne'er to know its like, 195
For others who judge me by their measure?
I will not pleasure them, deny my voice,
For beggars who wouldst fear atypic choice.
I could not give a fig for so-called populistic dread.
For we are in a state of bliss (and not a state of red). 200
I'll have this silken strand for she's my song.
And if love be the food of music, right on!
Besides, we kinda have to get married,
If thou dost get my drift. When dungeoning,
A forlorn spirit ofttimes needs a lift. 205

HAMEO
You mean she is with...uh...
(I really want to say child here, but...)

THELONIOUS
Grandchildern!!
Dost thou hear this, Lobster? Thou art to be an uncle.
Lymetrius, do demonstrate thy manners, thou wert bred. 210
Thou'st yet made known to me thy dear betrothed.
God rest her bones, she is the image of thy mother
(Less her limbs and seven stones). Why yea,
Thy nasal nymph doth have the faintest flush of nascency.
Dear cherub, with a kiss, I welcome thee unto our fold. 215
Now here's a hitch, the lady vanishes.

LYMETRIUS
Nobody move!!!

4.5 Hemlock accuses Lymetrius of evading his debt and demands his pound of flesh. Julinia convinces the magistrate that since the language of the agreement is vague it may be satisfied by "other means"—much to the displeasure of Hemlock. The magistrate marries both pair of lovers. Hippopotima laments her solitude but garners the affection of Fatstaff. The players bid all farewell and depart for Padua, lead by the amorous needs of Snuggy Bear. Schmuck discovers that his friend, the Muskrat, is female—and he, too, at long last, finds love.

---

2. **Here come the judge to fine my flippant friend:** Flip Wilson was known for his catchphrase "Here come da judge" on *Rowan & Martin's Laugh-In*, although the line was stolen from comedian Pigmeat Markham.

>   [*He looks for the hair, finding
>   it stuck to his father's lip.*]

Father,
Take heed. Thou wert well-nigh to eat my bride!

THELONIOUS
Nay son, I ne'er to thee would be so rude.   220
(The groom doth e'er have license to first dibs.)

HAMEO
Let acrimony ebb this joyous eve.
In matrimony, cleave unto thy bride
And at your side, I'll make my matching vows.
Now puck, go summon forth the magistrate,   225
That we be married 'fore the day grows late.

4.5   *Enter Hemlock, Magistrate,
             Fatstaff, Guildencrantz and Rosenstern.*

HEMLOCK
Allow me to oblige, my noble prince.
Here come the judge to fine my flippant friend,
The scofflaw who would skip out on his debt.

LYMETRIUS
My lord, I gainsay this fallacious claim.

MAGISTRATE
All asseveration shall be voiced   5
Before the law shall speak its choice.
Bring forth the witness to this murky pact.

FATSTAFF
Your honor, I didst hear the bargain struck.
And as a most esteemed libationist, bamboozlary
And whore-mongerer, my word is...up for sale in   10
Most affairs. But as for this, unsullied and unsold—
Unless...anyone?...no? The facts are these, my lord.
Lymetrius (henceforth referred to as exhibit A),
Anxious to annul a gambling loss, didst as an emptor
Shunned my caveat, and for this anthro-carnivore   15
(The villain of the second part) didst make a binding oath.
In recompense for two-fold thousand coins, the dinner,

29-30. **the maxims...I merely read the articles:** A men's magazine from the UK, now distributed online, Maxim is known predominantly for its photography of scantily clad actresses, singers and female models.

36. **the Cannibalistic Usurers of Europe:** Great group to join, but I hear the dues'll cost you an arm and a leg.

39. **Perfectly clear**: For a guy whose catchphrase was "Let me make one thing perfectly clear," Nixon sure spent a lot of time practicing the art of obfuscation.

>   Nay, defendant, wouldst provide
>   Remuneration or a pound of hide.

LYMETRIUS
>   I shan't refute the nature of my pledge
>   But I've yet nigh a fortnight to comply.

MAGISTRATE
>   And such would be the case but 'tis not so.
>   Prevailing laws this annum were revised
>   And do so state, when wager funds are loaned,
>   Recipients are landlocked by their zone
>   And deemed defaulters should they dare to stray
>   Beyond their region 'fore their debt's repaid.

HAMEO
>   Why this outlandish edict is absurd.

MAGISTRATE
>   I don't condone the maxims that are made,
>   I merely read the articles and then
>   Interpret and enforce what has been writ.
>   As for the founding of this statute here,
>   This litigant can certainly thank CUE.

HAMEO
>   Thank me?

MAGISTRATE
>   No CUE.
>   The lobby for the Cannibalistic Usurers of Europe—
>   They're quite an influential bunch, don't ya know.
>   At any rate, the law's...

KING MILHOUS
>   Perfectly clear.

MAGISTRATE
>   Lymetrius, accused, is guilty found.
>   The plaintiff may now fix upon his fee,
>   Show mercy and take payment plus his rate
>   Or, as renowned, a pound upon his plate.

45. **please sir, I want some Moor:** If you've never seen the 1968 film *Oliver!,* or at least read the book *Oliver Twist,* someone should slap the Dickens out of you.

48. **gonif:** (Yiddish) a disreputable or dishonest person.

52. **evince:** be evidence of; indicate

59. **perquisites:** something that is claimed as a right or privilege

HEMLOCK
Though some may deem me but a twisted cur,
I prithee, please sir, I want some Moor.

THELONIOUS
My son's a Moor? His mother quoth
They didst share both but a really good tan.

MAGISTRATE
The gonif, pardon, plaintiff hath spoken.
Now let him claim his just desserts.

LYMETRIUS
Hameo, canst thou not flex thy royal brawn?

HAMEO
To intercede wouldst crack the paradigm
And evince to the citizens that I'm no better
Than the vanquished tyrants felled.
So tristfully, eyes swelled, I must decline.

LYMETRIUS
Then 'pon my poor carnality he'll dine.

JULINIA
Wait! Good magistrate a word with thee.
Methinks for my concerns you'll find accord.
This pact was forged with vague phraseology.
Though Hemlock's due his fleshy perquisites,
Ne'er was it set the manner of redress
Nor that remittance metaphorical
Would not suffice to deem this rectified.

MAGISTRATE
My lady,
What would you advocate the court provide?

[*Julinia whispers in the Magistrate's ear.*]

Yea, it satisfies the terms, if not, intent.

HEMLOCK
Come, come. This legalese leaves me perturbed.
Let justice and Lymetrius be served.

74. **cock and bull:** There are several suggestions as to the origin of the phrase "cock and bull." One posits it derives from the name of two inns, The Cock and The Bull, in Stoney Stratford—a stopping-off point for travelers from London to the North of England. A rivalry grew between patrons of each, giving increasingly exaggerated and fanciful reports known as "cock and bull stories." Another claims it is from an old French folk tale about a magical rooster and jackass or "coq-a-l'âne," a term meaning "an incoherent story passed from one subject to another." Of course, in the 20th century and beyond it's known to just refer to straight-up "bullshit."

83-84. **by sword of Damocles I have been pricked:** As the story goes, an envious Damocles was allowed to switch places with King Dionysius for a day, but could only enjoy this majestic luxury upon a throne with a sword dangling above and held aloft by a single horsehair. The "pricked" part I will leave to your imagination.

MAGISTRATE
  Hemlock, is thy resolve unshakable?
  Wouldst thou not have thy monies and
  Forgo these damages? 70

HEMLOCK
  Dissuade me not, thou cunning magistrate.
  My chosen remedy is in our midst.
  I'll have my just forthcoming benefits.
  And spare me, if you please, the cock and bull.

MAGISTRATE
  Well, the bull anyway. Guards! 75
  Escort the plaintiff yonder out of sight
  So that this claim be settled out of court.

  *[The Guards take Hemlock
  off behind a partition.]*

LYMETRIUS
  Julinia, I am awash in bafflement.
  What murmurings made jurisprudence sway?
  And what amends, pray, do I owe this fiend? 80

  [Julinia whispers in Lymetrius's ear.]

LYMETRIUS
  O, 'tis quite a foul loophole to pass through.
  And yet a man must do what he must do.

  *[Lymetrius lowers his pants and joins
  Hemlock behind the partition.]*

HEMLOCK (*head protruding.*)
  What is this? By sword of Damocles
  I have been pricked. Ods Bodkins!!!

THELONIOUS
  Ewh, that's gotta hurt. 85

  Enter the Players.

HAMEO
  Ah, dear Players, I do laud ye for thy labors.

89. **My kingdom for a bitch:** In Shakespeare's *Richard III*, the titular king cries "A horse, a horse, my kingdom for a horse" upon the mortal wounding of his steed in battle. Of course, if you're willing to trade a kingdom for a bitch, you're probably, like, super horny.

96. **I'll bite your balls off**: Let a half witch near your balls at your own peril.

97. **piles:** could be a large amount of something or a fancy word for hemorrhoids—your call.

105. **Out damn Spot! Out I say!:** the guilt-ridden lament of Lady Macbeth, referring to the imaginary blood on her hands—not a dog.

TOP DOG
  My honor.

STARVIN' MARVIN
  My privilege.

SNUGGY BEAR
  My kingdom for a bitch.

HALF WITCH
  Psst. Yeah, down here! You lookin' for some of this? 90
  Thou knowest what they spake: "Once you go
  Black magic, you never go back."

SNUGGY BEAR
  Regrets to thee, little mama.
  Lord know'st I needs it bad, but...I ain't there yet.

HALF WITCH
  Hold me back. Hold me back. Come hither ya little... 95
  I'll bite your balls off.

  Hemlock and Guards reemerges.

HEMLOCK
  O, injustice hast been thrust towards me in piles.

HAMEO
  Thou wert whining for thy recompense, though reaped
  Comeuppance as thy bitter fruit.

HEMLOCK
  O, he didst comeuppanced me alright. 100
  I'll tell ya one thing, that was much more than a pound.

THELONIOUS
  Serves thee right and fie upon thee, wolf,
  Who wouldst ingurgitate my lone offspring.
  Sic 'im Lobster.

HEMLOCK (*to Lobster.*)
  Out damn Spot! Out I say! 105

  [*Exit Hemlock.*]

  Enter Lymetrius.

115-17. **brief candles...an idiot:** a play on a line from Shakespeare's *Macbeth*, "Out, out, brief candle! Life's but a walking shadow, a poor player that struts and frets his hour upon the stage and then is heard no more. It is a tale told by an idiot, full of sound and fury, signifying nothing." (Shakespeare was rarely invited to parties, being the Debbie Downer of his day.)

TOP DOG
Say, what's the score, my moor?

*Enter Rosenstern and Guildencrantz
unobtrusively.*

THELONIOUS
My child, thank the heavens thou art whole.
And though thy Mum deceived me this do know,
If thou art Moor, I love thee nonetheless.

LYMETRIUS
If thou wert sane, I could not love thee more. 110

[*Thelonious and Lymetrius embrace.*]

GUILDENCRANTZ (*sniffling*)
O, pop-and-sonly love doth choke me up.

ROSENSTERN (*sniffling*)
I never had the likeness as a pup.

TOP DOG (*to Rosenstern and Guildencrantz*)
Yo! Ain't you the—? Didn't we just—?

ROSENSTERN
Poor players, do not fret a bit
About brief candles being out or lit, 115
For as the buddhas say, life is but a herd of yesterdays
Staged by an idiot...or something like that.
But if concerned, consult with Whoositstern.

GUILDENCRANTZ
In faith, I was well christened Whatshiscrantz,
But have thy pick, all roses stinks the same. 120

TOP DOG
Oh never mind.

GUILDENCRANTZ
We never do.

HAMEO
And now good folk come forth and congregate.
Your honor, let our knots be firmly tied.
Espouse we mates unto our waiting brides. 125

126. **Marry:** used in several ways—listen; I agree; indeed; well—or as a pun

138. **Two gents who veer on a...uncharted lane:** a play on Shakespeare's *Two Gentlemen from Verona*

146. **lather, rinse, repeat:** keeps hair—including nostril hair—supple, manageable and health looking.

MAGISTRATE
Marry, I shall bestow the gift of wedlock presently.

[Hippopotima bursts into tears.]

FATSTAFF
Sweet maid, a handkerchief to dab the dew
From thy fair mountaintop.

HIPPOPOTIMA
Wherefore dost thou pour honey in my ears?

FATSTAFF
'Tis nectar that befits my king-sized queen. 130
Your fat enslaves me as thine humble drone.
I like a lass with mutton-laden bones.
And after this to-do, my XL-BBW,
Perchance thou'd deign have dinner at my hut.
We'll wine and dine and chew the you-know-what. 135

HIPPOPOTIMA
I could eat.

MAGISTRATE
Dear friends, the blessings of this day are heaven sent.
Two gents who veer on a strange uncharted lane
(Few navigate with half their wits and property retained)
Do each join with their chosen counterparts, 140
To share their hopes and slay their fears
And sate their pining hearts.
Hameo, Julinia, Lymetrius and hair apparent,
Art ye promiséd and by thine other bound by this conceit;
To honor, love and cherish, 145
To lather, rinse, repeat,
Till twilight's ebb
When earth doth serve ye
As thine humble bed?

HAMEO/JULINIA/LYMETRIUS
We do. 150

NOSTRIL HAIR (*voiced by anyone.*)
You betcha!

154. **the crazy stick:** a thin piece of wood that has fallen or has been cut from a crazy tree (If someone is hit with a crazy stick, they will become insane. Crazy sticks look very similar to ugly sticks, so do take care in evaluating these branches properly and select the one appropriate to your desired effect.)

157. **marriage-á-trois:** (French) when three sets of couples get married at the same time (It's considered one of the kinkiest ways to get hitched.)

164. **bafflegab:** like gobbledygook or rigamarole but more circumlocutory

MAGISTRATE
Then by the awesome and oft abuséd powers
Of the judiciary, I proclaim you man and dame,
And thee, utterly smited by the crazy stick,
Yet married all the same. 155

HIPPOPOTIMA
Perhaps we should have joined them in their pledge?

FATSTAFF
I'm not into a marriage-á-trois.

HAMEO
Dear witches, I would have a word with you.
One odd prognostication daunts me still.
I savvy, by your riddlings, 160
How my love wouldst wear the pants,
And he, Lymetrius, 'neath nose
Would findeth his romance.
Yet ponder as I may your bafflegab,
I can't infer how I would earn a throne 165
Yet ne'er a kingdom have to call my own?

FIRST WITCH
Then ope thy ears and clear the wax away.
Ne'er will thee call "a" kingdom home, 'tis true.

SECOND WITCH
For thou shalt rule no single realm...but two!

HALF WITCH
Semantics—heh, we get off on that shit. 170

TOP DOG (*rapping.*)
Prince Hameo,
On my behalf and of my crew,
We would extend to you
A hale and hearty salut.
So representin' us all, 175
To voice with deferential lip,
Here be our mighty, erudite-y,
Bard-ass brother, Q-Tip.

179. **eventide:** evening; **elatious nuptialities:** joyous marriage

180. **cusphold:** a portmanteau of the words *cusp* and *threshold*; **porpending monarchification:** upcoming coronation

181. **poetical fratagerie:** a brotherhood of poets; **utterate:** to express; convey in words

182. **appreciatude:** thankfulness; **flewcoupifying:** to release from confinement or custody; **dungivity:** imprisonment or captivity

183. **extagerant wedship:** rapturous wedding

184. **longeverous:** lengthy; abundant

188. **Come on and kiss me, Kate:** from the 1948 musical *Kiss Me Kate* and its source material, Shakespeare's *The Taming on the Shrew*

Q-TIP
  Unto ye, upon the eventide of your elatious nuptialities
  And the cusphold of your porpending monarchification,
  Our poetical fratagerie would like to utterate our
  Appreciatude for flewcoupifying us from dungivity
  And bid ye an extagerant wedship
  And a longeverous reign.

JULINIA
  I can for life not fathom what's been said.
  But players, have our thanks. Now off to bed.

HAMEO
  Why, there's a wench!
  Come on and kiss me, Kate...uh...Julinia.

JULINIA
  OK. Who the hell is Kate?

HAMEO
  Well...'twas for a time this girl in Padua,
  But trust me, she was a real bitch.

  [*They kiss.*]

SNUGGY BEAR
  Hear dat boys? Dere's bitches in Padua. We outta here.

  [*Exeunt the Players.*]

SCHMUCK (*aside.*)
  Well, my woodland pals,
  Seems all are sure to shortly getteth some.
  Save me, your chum and humble narrator.

MUSKRAT
  Eek. Eek-eek. Eek. Eek-ekk, eek.

SCHMUCK
  Well...do not misconstrue, my furballed friend.
  In faith, I am most flatteréd, indeed.
  But I, you see, swingeth not along that avenue.

MUSKRAT
  EEK. EEK. EEK-EKK. EEK-EEK. EEK!!

203-04. **hairy chicks...Europe:** Girls who don't shave their underarms are really the pits.

213. **slapping paws:** Clap, you animals!

218. **the play's the thing:** from Shakespeare's *Hamlet*

220. **Dionysus:** the Greek god of theatre; also the god of the vine, grape harvest, winemaking, fertility, ritual madness and religious ecstasy—but mostly theatre

SCHMUCK
> A thousand pardons, please, my muskratette.
> Who knew, that 'neath thy pelt did stir a girlish heart?

MUSKRAT
> You know, some guys have a thing for hairy chicks.
> I mean, we are in Europe aren't we?

SCHMUCK
> Forsooth, my hirsute cutie. 205
> And I shall surely make amends
> When curtain falls and play doth end.
> (*Aside.*) And so my friends, this brings us to our close.
> Do shed ye not a tear, for all good shows
> And those of ill must perish thus. 210
> Which this may be, the critics will discern.
> But if thy praise be earned, we prithee do take pause
> And lavish us with slapping paws.
> We pray ye gleaned a touch of worldly truths
> Betwixt frivolity and laughs. 215
> In faith, how could ye not take note,
> With such unsubtleties shoved down your throat.
> But the play's the thing,
> All else be free to swallow or to spit as you see fit.
> May Dionysus bless you, that ye should 220
> Spare your time and coinage with our troop.
> And speaking for us all, and this brash mischievous runt,
> I stoop to you, as we do make our final exeunt.

[Exeunt.]

Scene Change Music and Sound Effects

Act 1, Scene 1	Overtures (This Is It)
Act 1, Scene 2	Beetlejuice Theme
Act 1, Scene 2	Tower Bells SFX
Act 1, Scene 3	(I Can't Get No) Satisfaction
Act 1, Scene 3	Trumpet Flourish - Smoke on the Water
Act 1, Scene 3	Trumpet Flourish - Wind Beneath My Wings
Act 1, Scene 3	Star Trek Theme SFX
Act 1, Scene 4	Crazy
Act 1, Scene 4	Trumpet Flourish - Mammy
Act 1, Scene 5	Hall of the Mountain King
Act 2, Scene 1	If I Were a Rich Man/Elizabethan Serenade
Act 2, Scene 2	William Tell Overture/Morning
Act 2, Scene 3	Merry Melodies Theme
Act 3, Scene 1	Merry Melodies Theme
Act 3, Scene 1	Yakety Sax
Act 3, Scene 1	Darth Vader Theme
Act 3, Scene 2	Respect
Act 3, Scene 2	Bewitched Nose Twitch SFX
Act 3, Scene 3	Jailhouse Rock
Act 3, Scene 4	That's Entertainment
Act 3, Scene 4	Trumpet Flourish - Hail to the Chief
Act 4, Scene 2	Trumpet Flourish - There's No Business Like Show Business
Act 4, Scene 2	Parents Just Don't Understand (Rap)
Act 4, Scene 2	Gun Shot SFX
Act 4, Scene 2	Trumpet Flourish - Is You Is or Is You Ain't My Baby?
Act 4, Scene 3	Mannix Theme (Duel)
Act 4, Scene 5	Brush Up Your Shakespeare (Curtain Call)

The Mannix Jazz Duel

Amongst the memories of your life, there are probably a handful of moments that you hold especially dear and even now wash over you with an indescribable sense of joy. For me, one of these was sneaking out into the back of the house each night during *Bard's* run, and watching The Mannix Jazz Duel.

The theme to this 1967-1975 TV detective series was composed by Lalo Schifrin, who practically owned this era and was the genius behind the themes to *Bullitt*, *Cool Hand Luke*, *Starsky & Hutch* and of course, *Mission: Impossible*. For the longest time, I had also credited him with the amazing theme to the Buddy Ebsen vehicle, *Barnaby Jones,* but later found that this signature piece should rightfully be attributed to Jerry Goldsmith—my sincere apologies to you, sir.

If you care to, I'm sure the melody is available on YouTube for your listening pleasure. Fortunately, I was able to find a version with a slightly less frantic tempo which lent itself more gracefully as the backdrop to this mortal confrontation.

Would that I could have had you by my side to witness this wonderful absurdity or that my descriptive powers could coax these meager pages to transport you now to that bygone place and time. Yet, I will vainly attempt to offer you an inkling of a few choice moments of choreography that tickled me most particularly.

After several thrusts and parries, Hameo knocks Bolingbras's sword from his hand. As they struggle for control of the remaining sword—the music being written in 3/4 time—they break into a waltz, with a spin-out and return spin into a romantic dip.

As the two engage blades back and forth, Bolingbras's servant arrives with tea. Without stopping, Bolingbras indicates his request for two lumps of sugar, the tea is poured and he enjoys his refreshment while Hameo maintains his ineffective attack. Then Bolingbras takes a phone call and tells the servant on the line to make sure to pick up some eggs and milk, before returning his full attention to the battle.

Later, Bolingbras gains the advantage, advancing on Hameo as both disappear off-stage while two other actors—dressed identically—appear on the opposite side of the stage, continuing the exchange of blows until the tide turns and "Hameo" forces "Bolingbras" from the stage and the original actors reemerge.

In the last moments of the duel, Bolingbras smacks Hameo on the back of the head, sending him into a somersault onto the ground. As the king approaches for the coup de grâce, he is suddenly run through by Hameo at the last musical crescendo and drops defeated on the final downbeat of the piece.

Well, there's a little taste of what you might have seen upon a stage on a fall evening in New York City many years ago. Perhaps one day you will be able to enjoy the full experience during a long-awaited revival performance—but I would exactly hold your breath on that one.

In Defense of Satire and Freedom of Language

Congratulations! You've made it to the end and are *still reading*—amazing! Honestly, I didn't know if you would make it this far, and yet, despite all my concerns, here you are. You know, a few things have been weighing on my mind lately that I would love to discuss with you. Can we talk? Actually, I'd be doing most of the talking (or in this case, writing) given the conversational limitations of the written page—hope that's not a problem. Anyway, pull up a chair, crack open a beer and let's get started.

I realize you don't know me very well, but if you've finished *A Bard's Day's Night*, you must know this: I love words. I love the sound of them; the way they feel coming out of my mouth; their arrangement and interplay, harmony and discordance, meanings and origins. Words are "the bomb"—and have the explosive force to change minds, bring tears of laughter or sorrow, educate or obfuscate, destroy lives or enrich them. They can be a Molotov cocktail tossed into the heart of a crowd or a hopeful daisy slipped gently into the barrel of a soldier's gun, depending on the mind from which they pour.

I fancy myself, first and foremost, an entertainer. I enjoy nothing more than coming up with unusual concepts that amuse me, sharing them with you and putting a smile on your face—I mean, what artist finishes a work and says, "Boy, I really hope this pisses a lot of people off and they all hate me"? However, that's a risk I'm willing to take since, for me, laughter is not enough. I like questioning social conventions, challenging beliefs and provoking thoughts about where things fall on the moral spectrum. Without these elements, I'd be no more than a stand-up regaling you with a droll observational tale regarding an anthropomorphized sock escaping my dryer.

Sadly, I have noticed in recent years, society is becoming increasingly segmented. Those that used to champion individuality are now affixing labels *to themselves*, joining groups (physically or digitally) that are bound by like-minded views, and railing against anyone that may threaten their belief systems. We have a consortium of gun-toting, god-fearing, gay-hating, border-patrolling, climate-denying, abortion-thwarting, civil war-reenacting grand old tea partiers in an existential deathmatch with tree-hugging, sex-changing, immigrant-loving, fetus-killing, black-lives-mattering, bullet-limiting, science-believing, bleeding heart donkeys; and in the process, we have lost something very important. We have lost *our sense of humor*.

Comedians say they can no longer play college campuses and certain venues because audiences are too sensitive or easily offended, taking a zero-tolerance stance on any jokes that might seem to belittle a protected class or cause. Don't get me wrong; we have some very serious issues out there: Neo-Nazis hate groups, mass shootings, gay discrimination, race/gender pay inequities, black people killed by bigoted or overzealous police officers, xenophobic deportations, attacks at abortion clinics. But audiences need to be able to discern between someone trampling on their values, and someone who is trying to release some air from this enormous pressure value called life. Busting balls is a far cry from cracking skulls—some either cannot or choose not to make that distinction. We may one day solve these seemingly intractable societal ills, but making levity taboo will not be part of that solution.

In this play, I have an entire section dedicated to exploring the issue of excessive sensitivity in which, as a device, I used a lot of racial epithets. Was it because I hate all manner of ethnicities and want each eradicated from the face of the earth? No, actually I really don't have any problem with people that differ from myself and avoid biases as best I can. Unfortunately, it's hard to be a human being without developing some preconceived notions about people—and what is a prejudice really but the drawing of a conclusion based on past experience—it's actually kinda like science. So allow me now to cop to the following societal pet peeves: When I'm taking the subway in New York, I find that I am invariably perturbed by young black kids with loud boomboxes, old Asian women shouting their conversation like the other one is completely deaf, and religious nuts using this cylindrical aluminum conveyance we're all trapped in as their personal underground cathedral for the express purpose of informing me that I'm going to hell. That's it. Basically, my issues are all decibel related. It's not about race, color or creed. It's about rude, loud and annoying. Be chill on the subway...and we cool.

One of the epithets used in this play—and arguably the most infamous one—is the dreaded N-word. As a logophile, I have always been fascinated by the notion that there could be a word that everyone knows, everyone has said at least once, but is considered so vile and abhorrent that it must never be uttered in polite society—unless, of course, you're black and then you can say it all day long. Really? Come on, black folk! What am I supposed to say when somebody asks me what my favorite hip hop group is? *N-Words Wit Attitude*?

You've got to realize that if you tell me there's a word in the English language that I am categorically forbidden to say, you're practically *begging me* to say it. Of course, this is all purely academic, as I really have no use whatsoever for the N-word or any other racial slur in my personal life, employing them rarely, comedically and never in anger. But I realize this isn't the case with everyone and true bigots go well beyond words. After slavery, segregation, police brutality, job inequality and racism, do black people have a legitimate beef about their treatment in America? Abso-fucking-lutely! Should they then at least be allowed to control the use of a derogatory slur? Even in the face of such atrocities, my reply must be: No way, José! Butterflies are free, and so are words (even the naughty ones). Ban one and just wait to see what's banned next. Can anyone say "slippery slope"? Please don't—so overused!

If all this is leaving you a tad despondent, what you may be missing, as many do, is the rarely explored upside to hate-speech. (What!?!) So if you will, let me take that frown and turn it upside down. Since it's widely known that all white people look alike, letting them say the N-word immediately grants you the ability to tell the good ones from the assholes. It's like having a fucking superpower—without the hassle of flying to Wakanda for a Vibranium-laced herb shot.

But seriously folks, we really do need to get passed our intolerance—of those that differs from ourselves, and equally important, for that which offends us. If here, in the conquest of this goal, I have perturbed you in any way, please do not think me an animal. "I'm just a soul whose intentions are good. Oh Lord, please don't let me be misunderstood."

Allow me now to make mention of another interesting word-related controversy that I feel is completely retarded. That's right, the use of the word *retarded*. You may recall from your schoolyard days the sophisticated use of this particular barb in a heated battle of wits—"You're retarded." "No, *you're* retarded." What I have never heard of is someone sauntering up to a mentally challenged person, getting right up in their face and saying "Hey, ya fuckin' retard. How'd you get so fucking retarded, you stupid retarded fuck? Having trouble with two plus two? It's four, ya dumb tard. Well, gotta go. Good luck with all that retardedness, ya stupid, dumb fuckin' retard!" This never happens—*never*! Find me the guy doing this and I will personally put a bullet in his head. This term is only ever used colloquially to refer to someone who is in full possession of all their faculties but may have made an intellectual blunder or to some situation that seems completely illogical. No one but a truly vile human being is using the word towards, or in the vicinity of, people with actual mental disabilities. Yet, that doesn't seem to stop self-appointed firemen from the 451Word Brigade from protecting the inflamed ears of the sensitive from the non-existent threat that is the R-word.

Now, let me provide for you the irony of all linguistic ironies. The following are terms previous used to refer to a person with cognitive impairments: *idiot*, *imbecile*, *moron*, *feeble-minded* and *slow*. Each, in their day, perfectly acceptable terms to describe the mentally challenged. Each in succession, supplanting its antecedent in a quest to find a kinder, gentler means of addressing an unfortunate condition. Until, around 1895, when a new term came into the popular lexicon. A beautiful, lyrical word that would replace all the divisive and derisive expressions that had come before. The word was *retarded*—from the Latin *retardare*, meaning "to make slow, delay, keep back or hinder." For lovers of music, when a composer requires a particular passage to be played at a slackened tempo it is indicated in the orchestration as a *retard*.

And all was well throughout the land, until June 23rd, 1958, when Tommy Milsap of Goose Creek, South Carolina saw a classmate on the playground trip on his shoelace and do a faceplant on the tetherball court and exclaimed for all the world to hear, "Nice going, ya fuckin' retard!" And with that, the quest for a more compassionate nomenclature began anew.

Words, my friends, are innocent. It's the origins of hatred that needs to be addressed—not vocabulary. Someone could say "I love you, my nigga" or "Hey boys, let's tie that African American to the back of my trailer hitch." What's more important, the terminology or the sentiment? Ban a word and someone surely will devise or transform another to take its place. Do you think a person with *special needs* will be magically shielded by this sympathetic term? I'm sure Tommy Milsap's grandson is already at work to undermine it. "Hey, you're one of those 'special needs' kids, right? How's it going, Speshy? You like being special there, Spesh? Love that crayon drawing you got going there. It's *spesh*tacular!"

You may note that in the title of this essay I did not call for freedom of speech, but rather, freedom of *language*. To my mind, you should not only be permitted to say what you want, but choose, without reprisal, the specific words that best suit the message you want to convey. Denying this fundamental right would be like the Paint Nazi barging in on the creation of *Starry Night*, ripping the brush from Van Gogh's hand and shouting "No yellow for you!"—an audience cutting off its own collective ear to spite its face. Writers, satirists and comedians must always have the full palette of expression at their disposal. Any attempt at controlling language to appease the perpetually offended is something I would have to consider—hmm, what's the word I'm looking for here?—*retarded*.

In regards to satire, one employs irony and exaggeration to expose vice, hypocrisy, and folly—often by devising scenarios that are *contrary* to their actual values.

There is a well-known Academy Award winning film depicting the inhuman brutality of concentration camps in Germany during World War II. Did anyone turn to Steven Spielberg after seeing that film and say, "Wow, Steve! Never realized you were such an anti-Semite"? Of course not.

Barbarism was on full display for one very simple reason—you can't make *Schindler's List* without Nazis. And you can't ridicule human foibles without demonstrating them.

Unfortunately, the PC Gestapo either doesn't grasp that or feels the harm it may inflict upon the delicate sensibilities of viewers does not justify a parable's message. Well, I can certainly tell you this: I have never judged someone by the color of their skin; but I do judge them by the thickness of it. Islamic fundamentalist kill people over cartoons of Mohammed. We're not there—yet, but is that the direction we really want to go? To those who feel they must ensure a "safe space" for fragile snowflakes, I would ask—as I paraphrase a spicy old Captain Morgan ad—"Got a little Islamic fundamentalist in you?"

These days no one is paranoid without reason. There are a lot of bad people in the world with bad motives and they might be coming to get you. So be strong and fight your battles—but know who your real enemies are. Believe it or not, those whose stock-in-trade is comedy and satire are usually on your side. So heed this worthy advice from a wile old fox: If someone is lampooning you and mocking all the values you hold most dear, take a deep breath—he might just be a satirist.

Despite what you may believe, viewing someone's work doesn't necessarily provide you with some magical Kaufmanesque portal into the inner workings of their mind. Who knows best the secret behind Mona Lisa's smile—you or DaVinci? But if you'd like to know who I am and where I'm coming from, let me tell you. I am a time traveler, and I come from a fantastic future many millennia from now; where as sovereign individuals, we abandon groupthink; do not impose our values on others; can hear and perhaps even learn from alternate viewpoints; and revel in our diversity. Most importantly, we know how to *take a fucking joke*. We're secure enough to be able to razz and tease and kid around with one another and everybody's OK with it. And when the joke's on us, we smile, give a wink and a little elbow nudge, and say, "Hey, good one." So, jump in your DeLorean, get your flux capacitor fluxing and come join us here, won't you? It's a wonderful time to be alive!

As the late Rodney King once asked, "Can't we all just get along?" Well, perhaps not yet, Rodney. But in the meantime, can't we all just have a laugh?

www.ingramcontent.com/pod-product-compliance
Lightning Source LLC
Chambersburg PA
CBHW030310080526
44584CB00012B/516